# Exploring the Marquesas Islands

Fine Edge
Productions

**Joe Russell**

Published by
Fine Edge Productions
13589 Clayton Lane
Anacortes, Washington 98221

Library of Congress Cataloging-in-Publication Data
Russell, Joe, 1947 -
    Exploring the Marquesas Islands / by Joe Russell.
    p.    cm.
    Includes bibliographical references and index.
    ISBN 0-938665-64-2
    1. Marquesas Islands (French Polynesia) 2. Russell, Joe, 1947---Journeys--Marquesas
    Islands (French Polynesia) 3. Sailing--Pacific Ocean. I. Title.
    DU700 .R87 1999
    996.3'1--dc21                                                99-053080

IMPORTANT LEGAL DISCLAIMER
This book is designed to provide experienced skippers with planning information for cruising the Marquesas Islands. Every effort has been made, within limited resources, to make this book complete and accurate. There may well be mistakes, both typographical and in content; therefore, this book should be used only as a general guide, not as the ultimate source of information on the areas covered. Much of what is presented in this book is local knowledge based upon personal observation and is subject to human error.

The author and publishers assume no liability for errors or omissions, or for any loss or damage incurred from using this information.

Printed in Canada.

Cover and book design:    Pamela Hidaka Design
Production and  illustration graphics:    Pamela Hidaka Design
Map graphics:    Michael Victor & Pamela Hidaka Design
Text photos and hand sketches:    Joe Russell
Editing:    Réanne Hemingway-Douglass, Elayne Wallis, and Pamela Hidaka

*To Capt. Fritz Seyfarth, a true sailorman who cast off for the ultimate "adventure under a spread of sail."*

*To Captains Bill and Patsy Bolling, your adventures past, present and future are what keep us all going.*

*To Mom and Dad, who always made sure that my life was an adventure.*

*To Hannah and Garrett Murray. At all costs, live your dreams of adventure.*

## Joe Russell

Joe Russell grew up in the San Francisco Bay area, where he attended Cal State Hayward. After being injured in a hydroplane accident, he took to sailing on the bay which, in 1968, led to a yacht delivery job to the Virgin Islands where he set up residence. While living in the Caribbean, Joe sailed to most of the countries of Central and South America. Joe's articles on Central America have been featured in Cruising World magazine. Joe currently lives in Half Moon Bay, California with his wife and first mate, Mary. He is the father of four and a recent grandfather of twins.

# Contents

# Foreword

Ever since I've known him, Joe Russell and his book have been inseparable. I first met them both in 1994, in Rosalie's restaurant in Hakahau Valley, Ua Pou, where Joe was comfortably ensconced, sipping a beer and working away on his draft. A year or so later, we met again in Hawaii, where he showed me a manuscript that had grown to surprising proportions. Along with the detailed narrative descriptions and sketches of anchorages which one would expect in a cruising guide, Joe had added information on Marquesan geology, wildlife, culture, and archeology in an effort to make the work a one-volume compendium for cruisers with diverse interests. At our meeting in Kaneohe, a place which rather forcibly recalls the humid Marquesan environment, we went over several aspects of Marquesiana and discussed his plans for further work and ultimate publication. After that, I was off again to the Marquesas and other parts of the Pacific, and I temporarily lost touch with Joe. Then, one night in 1998, the phone rang in my Alexandria residence and it was Joe, still working on his book; he'd tracked me down through an e-mail service and informed me that he'd also ended up in northern Virginia, about 30 miles from where I live.

This might seem like a coincidence, but it's actually a rather common occurrence for those who are bitten by the "Marquesas bug," that non-fatal, decidedly benevolent malady that links all true lovers of the exotic and wildly beautiful archipelago and its people. We're a very diverse lot in terms of professional background, interests, politics, religion, or whatever dimension you select, but we're united by our dominating fascination with the Marquesas and all things Marquesan. We know about each other, maintain loose contact, and somehow keep running into one another in rather unusual places. (The strangest encounter for me was at the head of a line for the "gentleman's facilities" at London Heathrow Airport bright and early one chilly morning where I recognized a yachtsman I'd met 30 years previously.) The Marquesas have seen some of the greatest names of western maritime history, art, and literature, pass through the archipelago. Many of these figures have been smitten by the islands: feisty little Commodore Davy Porter, U.S. Navy, whose fascination with his Marquesans allies and adversaries radiates through the pages of a combat cruise journal; Herman Melville, who never quite recovered from his contacts with the lovely Marquesan girls; Adm. Count Maximilian von Spee, leading his Asiatic squadron to its doom at the Falklands, but still consumed with the beauty of the Nuku Hiva landscape; and of course, Paul Gauguin, the would-be "savage" who came seeking a savage sanctuary in which to spend his last agonizing and lonely days, are but a few. The Marquesas have also attracted their share of anthropologists and archeologists like myself, for whom the Marquesan past and Marquesan culture and language offer intriguing clues to more fully reveal that greatest of all wonders of the ancient world — the settlement of Polynesia.

For many years the relative isolation of the Marquesas kept away visitors but now that isolation has been broken thanks to Air Tahiti, the *Aranui*, and the expansion of yachting activity. Regrettably, however, most of these visitors see the Marquesas as merely another remote set of volcanic islands, known only from a quick skim through a superficial tourist guidebook or a glance at Melville's *Typee* (which is not exactly current intelligence). For such visitors, including many yachtspeople, the islands are initially impressive, but there are too many inconvenient features among which the most important are annoying sand flies, rough terrain and a poor road network. The Marquesas soon becomes just another set of islands that have to be endured for as brief a period as possible. One drops in *en route* to somewhere else just to have one's "ticket punched" (and buy the T-shirt), get some gas or diesel fuel, load up with water, and then split for the coral atolls of the Tuamotu archipelago or the enticements of Tahitian fleshpots (enticements which, incidentally, are most attractive when seen from afar). And anyway, as a number of visitors have remarked: "There's really not much to see there...!"

Joe Russell's book, so laboriously composed over these last several years, is dedicated to proving precisely the opposite of that brain-dead and typically touristic assertion. This comparatively tiny and isolated archipelago supports an incredibly rich bounty for the natural historian: geology, marine and land flora and fauna; archeology, ethnology, and language, all waiting to be sampled and enjoyed. Joe has done a great job of assembling the information necessary to appreciate the Marquesas. Using this guide, the visitor to the Marquesas is limited only by his or her interests, skill, and energy. Of course, you have to get off your duff to experience all that, because most of the interesting sights and sites can be reached only through some physical exertion (often involving a bit of excitement or risk!) There are no theme parks, as yet, in the Marquesas. You'll also have to exert a little effort to get to know the Marquesans (just as you would with new neighbors in, let's say, Dubuque, Iowa) but all such efforts will be well rewarded, because there is no truer friend than a Marquesan friend.

Joe wants to convince yachtspeople, as well as those arriving by other modes of transport, that the Marquesas are not merely a nautical stopover on the way to "attractions" of other islands but could, and should, be thought of as a destination in their own right. Despite the depredations of European contact, there is still much that survives of the Marquesan culture beside its sonorous language, which is so different from Tahitian in intonation and stress. A cultural renaissance is underway; the old performing arts, tattooing, bone carving and bark-cloth (tapa)-making are

flourishing again, reinvigorated by new technology (tattoo needles fashioned from electric razors have replaced the old bone needle-and-hammer technique) and the availability of early western anthropological studies which preserved design elements that otherwise would have been long forgotten. In this regard, the Marquesas contrast sharply with Tahiti, where much of what is peddled as "native" or "traditional" culture is, in fact, "borrowed" from other unsuspecting Pacific peoples most importantly, from the Marquesans! Tahitians have long since appropriated the Marquesan tiki form and Marquesan tattoo design motifs and, in recent years, have lifted some of the Marquesan dances and dance steps labelling them as their own.

I hope that Joe's persevering efforts will succeed in inducing his fellow yachtsmen and all other tourists to tarry a while in the many pleasant bays of the Marquesas, to explore the landscape, meet the people and prove for themselves that this remote seat of an ancient and brilliant culture holds the stuff of which enduring memories are made. Perhaps you too will be bitten by the "bug!"

*Robert C. Suggs*
*Alexandria, Virginia*

**Editor's Note:**
Archaeologist Robert Suggs is a world-renowned authority on the Marquesas Islands. Please refer to Recommended References for his most noted works.

# Preface

As a destination, the Marquesas are a unique cruiser's paradise. Few tourists ever go there by air since there is no official port of entry into French Polynesia. That distinction is reserved for Tahiti. It also costs more to fly to the Marquesas from Papeete, Tahiti 700 miles SE, than it does to fly to Papeete from Los Angeles. Therefore, most of the people who arrive in the Marquesas are sailors—or at least they are by the time they arrive. The trade winds vary from SE to NE, and since gentlemen (and gentleladies) never sail to weather, cruisers usually don't arrive from the west. (I am in awe of those who do.) For most of the 250-300 boats jumping off for the South Pacific each year, whether sailing from California 2,800 miles northeast, Panama or Costa Rica 3,600 miles east, or the Galapagos 3,000 miles due east, the first landfall is probably the Marquesas Islands.

Surprisingly, many of these sailors end up cruising on tighter schedules than they had working at home after spending years saving for the voyage of a lifetime. The American cruisers I've met in the Marquesas felt pressure to leave quickly to meet self-imposed deadlines. Rather than serving as a quick stopover, I propose that the Marquesas are a destination unto themselves that deserve the same scrutiny normally afforded the Society Islands, Tonga or New Zealand. From tiny Eiao in the northwest to rolly Vaituha to Hana Vave on mysterious Fatu Hiva 190 miles southeast, the Marquesas provide one of the most interesting, dramatic, and convenient cruising grounds in the world.

The more than 25 obvious anchorages (and the countless not-so-obvious gunkholes) offer more than a cruiser could visit during a short six-month stay. There are few, if any, anchorages requiring special care to enter. The bays are open, reef-free coves. Where coral reefs occur, they are invariably close to the beach and offer no danger to the cruising yacht. The reefs are primarily hazardous as a outboard prop-killer while taking a dinghy to shore and back.

Unlike some cruising areas, there are spectacular reasons to explore inland sites. Fascinating archeological digs, Vaipo waterfall at Hakaui, Vai'e'enui Falls at Hana Vave, the *ma* pits at Hanamenu—the largest ancient stone tiki in French Polynesia at Puamau—are just a few of the on-shore treats awaiting the intrepid cruiser. The varying geological and botanical faces of these islands run the gamut from Baja California deserts on the lee sides to sultry Sadie Thompson-style jungle landscapes. Breathtaking 2,000-foot vertical spires give way to rolling hills replete with wild pigs and goats.

With all these advantages plus no hurricanes, it makes sense to spend a first season exploring the Marquesas, winter in Hawaii then cruise back down the next season to continue your tour of the South Pacific and beyond. Once you get downwind of any destination, you will probably not look forward to a return beat to windward.

However, the volcanic tropical beauty and the ease of navigation within the Marquesas are not the islands' greatest assets—its people are. A most generous and content population resides here. Except for a Peruvian "blackbirding" raid in the middle of the 19th Century, the Marquesans have never been subjected to slavery. The Marquesans carry no chips on their shoulders and they presume friendship with everyone. Proud of their history, they are always happy to discuss the legends and traditions of Fenua Enata—"The Land of Man"—that exist in their native language.

Strolling along at sundown listening to the small Marquesan ukeleles played by the teenagers is a special treat. This is not a show for tourists but the normal nightly activities of the young. Every edible item on the island is prepared and eaten with enthusiasm. The cuisine from *poisson cru* to *popoi*, *chèvre au-lait-coco* to breadfruit is delicious and easy to find and prepare.

These are the reasons I wrote this book. After having cruised virtually all the islands in the Caribbean and a lot of others, the Marquesas are among the finest cruising destinations I've ever sailed. Use this book as an hors d'oeuvre. It is intended to whet your appetite for these dramatic and mysterious islands. The diagrams included here detail anchorages and shore-side points of interest as I found them. The mythology and history, freely intermingled by Marquesans, were garnered from many sources. Books and interviews with local historians were invaluable. When I found that historians had different views, I chose the rendition that struck my fancy or sounded most reasonable.

I hope every visitor to *Fenua Enata* finds a secret place I have not discovered. There are many. I will be happy if you send me a report and a snapshot or two but if you keep your secret coves to yourself, I understand. The Marquesas are one place you can still visit and say you got there before it was too late.

## A Note on Place Names

Identifying the correct place names in the Marquesas is a shell game. The names are written differently from chart to chart; pronounced differently from island to island and language to language. The French as do the Spanish, do not believe that the letter "H" is worth pronouncing. Further, they add this poor letter to the beginning of some words in a willy-nilly fashion. The island Fatu Hiva is often pronounced by Marquesans as Fatu Iva. On the other hand, Nuku Hiva is always pronounced with a strong "H" sound.

Some more examples:

The title *Anse* ("cove" in French) is given to double-coved Anse Désanis on Tahuata. Hapatoni and Hana Tefau (sometimes and probably correctly written Te Fau) are the Marquesan names of the baylets within Anse Desanis.

Daniel's Bay, so named by American cruisers, is in fact Hakatea; Hana Iapa on Hiva Oa is sometimes spelled as one word; Baie de Controleur is pure French but is at the foot of one of the most famous valleys in the archipelago, Taipivai. This was the home of the Taipi tribe. Should the name of the valley be written Taipi Vai? Probably, but few do.

I bring this subject up not to educate but to beg the reader's pardon if, when they arrive, they find slight spelling or language differences from this text. Many centuries of culture shock and language variables have wreaked havoc on the reliability of place names. Of course, there's also that one cruising guide that has continued for years to label Hana Tefau, Hana Tefua. Phooey!

# Intro-
# duction

"Are you really going
out there in that?"

My road to the Marquesas was a long one. Thirty years cruising the Pacific from San Francisco to Panama, the Caribbean from Honduras' lovely Bay Islands to Trinidad-Tobago had instilled in me a sense of what paradise should be. The Caribbean from British Virgin Islands down through Grenada before the 1970s was pretty close to Nirvana for sailors. Some of us who sailed the Caribbean in those days lamented the necessary controls over cruising yachts and the unnecessary pollution of beautiful islands and looked for alternatives. The western Caribbean islands of Providencia and San Andres were investigated but, alas, we were too late, the time-share condos were already under construction.

The early 1990s found me in Golfito, Costa Rica one day, discussing with Roy Starkey (*S/V Sea Loone*) the relative merits of the Caribbean versus the South Pacific and points west. His descriptions convinced me that Horace Greeley was correct: While I was still young enough, I would "go West." When I mentioned running down the Mexican Coast as a shakedown cruise, Roy was blunt in his indignation. He said that I would waste valuable time and money on the Mexican Riviera while the charms of the South Pacific were drawing farther and farther away. He pointed out that by the time I reached Panama City, I would be 1,000 miles farther from the first Polynesian landfall than I was when tied up in Marina del Rey. On top of that, the tradewinds that usually start pumping at around 25°N, become flakey and affected by the Intertropical Convergence Zone between 10°N and 10°S. This makes a 45-day doldrum-ridden voyage from Panama to the Marquesas not unusual.

Roy convinced me. I decided on the spot to jump off from the West Coast and sail directly to the Marquesas Islands in French Polynesia. After few days of rest there we'd be off to Bora Bora via the Tuamotus. After that, the Cooks, Tonga and New Zealand while we waited out the hurricane season. Then we would continue the circumnavigation via Thailand and, finally to my personal target, Cocos Keeling in the Indian Ocean. The only detail remaining was to get a new boat.

I first saw *Christina* (formerly *Andiamo*) a bit more than a year before my proposed sailing date; she was in a slip in San Diego next to the departure end of the Lindbergh Field. She was so covered in spent jet fuel that walking on her decks left black shoe prints. She was a bare-bones DownEaster 38 with no equipment except an inoperative Adler-Barbour refrigerator, a cheap and broken windlass, and a functioning but older Loran unit, which would, of course, be useless offshore. But, she was clean inside with a dusty dry bilge and, best of all, she had less than 100 original hours on a four-cylinder Universal diesel. The sails, though 10 years old, were still waxy-new.

The time spent "building" a boat up to cruising standards is always an enjoyable period. With a lot of help from French friends, I rebuilt and installed a Monitor self-steering unit that had been salvaged by Roy Starkey from a boat that was wrecked on the rocks on the Pacific side of Panama. Installation of a 12 volt engine-driven cold plate refrigeration system from Randy Simkins and Joe Jeffers at Technautics was easy and never let us down. An extra line of reef points were sewn into the main and the sails were inspected and strengthened where necessary. A brand new hand-held Trimble GPS joined my old sextant to round out the navigation suite. I had no SSB or HAM radio transmitter aboard but I did have an intermittantly functioning VHF, an Icom handheld VHF, and a small multi-ban receiver that was our link to the world's news. An EPIRB was part of the abandon-ship bag and extra water and fuel were stored on deck. A reliable but noisy 20-amp wind generator helped two 5-amp solar panels keep the five deep-cycle 120 amp marine batteries topped off.

During this happy time, I met a very funny guy I'll call Elliot. He is the owner of a successful business in Los Angeles and bought his first (and probably last) two boats on the same day just before turning 60. One was a black-and-white nine-foot fiberglass runabout with a 30-horse Johnson on the stern. To match the runabout, he purchased a brand new 49-foot, slab-sided, three-story, twin-dieseled gin palace which never was named. The smaller boat was used almost exclusively for acrobatics inside Marina del Rey for the express purpose of annoying humorless live-aboards, while the larger one became a weekend cabin that occasionally waddled over to Catalina and back. The runabout and its cetacean slipmate were moored on Palawan Way close to the Del Rey Yacht Club where Elliot was waiting for a slip to open up.

*Christina* bobbed next to the sea wall in a slip across from Elliot's unnamed yacht. Every weekend while we were working on the boat, Elliot would drop by to see how the work was proceeding. After a beer or two and regaling *Christina's* crew with his latest adventure of getting lost returning from Catalina, Elliot would gesture toward the little cutter and utter the inevitable, "Are you really going out there in that?"

I could never convince Elliot that a month-long, non-stop passage to the Marquesas is not an unusual occurance nowadays especially with the advent of the GPS. "Why don't you go down the Mexican coast then quickly jump like a rabbit over to the South Pacific?" he asked. Well, I had been to Mexico many times and, second, every mile down the Mexican coast takes *Christina* a quarter of a mile farther away from Nuku Hiva.

Shaking his head, Elliot would reboard his woodless, chromed unnamed clorox bottle to mix a new batch of Bloody Marys and watch TV. Elliot is one of the most generous and entertaining people I have ever met and I imply no criticism of his boating lifestyle. As we all know, any boating is better than no boating. But the perception that long-distance cruising always carries undue risks is nonsense.

To paraphase an overused axiom, the three most important aspects of world voyaging are planning, planning, and planning. My crew selection was automatic; no planning was necessary there. Mary Hudecz Strahan had sailed with me in the Caribbean for years. Without her, the trip never would have taken place. And with her, this trip was everything a sailor could want.

We canned a lot of chicken and beef/pork meatballs and stocked the boat so well that two years later we still had some of the original stores. After a few hundred hours of sewing, painting and tending to details, the boat was polished, the brightwork shone and we were ready.

The *Christina* set sail in early January. We made the mistake of agreeing to buddy boat with a French couple in a 39-foot kitboat (which we dubbed *Porktown*) that wouldn't do 5 knots if it was pushed out of an airplane. *Christina* is a big, fat, seakindly cruising boat that never saw 9 knots but she was still faster than *Porktown*. No matter how good it sounds, I don't recommend buddy boating. I calculate that if we hadn't honored this ill-fated Franco-American alliance, we would have made the trip in 26 days instead of 31.

Throughout the entire 31 days, we had only two where the main was fully set. I can't count the number of times I shook out a reef only to reset it within an hour or so. This procedure became so common that I gave up and the standard sail arrangement became a double-reefed main, working jib and staysail. One reason that we carried so little main was that the *Monitor's* self-steering unit demands a balanced rig and if too much main is showing, the weather helm overwhelms the power of the vane gear. The wind piped daily up to 35 knots from the northeast and often topped 40 knots just before sundown. We never varied from a starboard tack on a course of 210°. From the time we passed Isla Guadalupe off the coast of Baja, we began calling the vane gear, "St. Monitor."

The crossing was the most pleasant of times. We crossed the equator on my birthday and had only four hours in the doldrums (ITCZ). As for my selection of crew, I could not have been luckier. Now that I think about it, however, I wonder who selected whom. Mary was the perfect shipmate. No matter how long or how hard it blew, there was always her happy, pleasant countenance looking back at me; I could count on it. Whether warranted or not, she always had confidence in my ability to carry us though. Never a cross word passed her lips the entire trip even though, I found out later, she felt profound trepidation over being offshore for so long.

Arrival day was spooky and mysterious. We started slowing the boat down two days prior to arrival so that we would not arrive in the middle of the night. Dawn broke on the 31st day at sea but no islands were to be found. At 7:00 a.m. it was broad daylight to our night-adjusted eyes and Nuku Hiva, our target, was still not visible. We were supposed to be only five miles away from a monstrous green island. I wanted to tap on the ol' GPS like we tap an errant barometer to level it. I pulled out the sextant as if to double check my position (it's hard to do a noon site at 7:00 a.m.) when the shoreline of Nuku Hiva became visible under the only cloud in the sky. Then the top of Eiao was barely visible many miles to starboard and we knew we had made it.

Christina

Three hours later we were anchored peacefully in Taiohae Bay but we remained onboard until the next day. The experience of arrival and lack of motion was a bit of a shock to our systems. Even the primitive and friendly island of Nuku Hiva seemed like a teeming anthill of civilization compared to our regular offshore routine.

The trip stats:
Total time of crew steering the boat: 8 hours.
Total engine-on time: 10 hours.
Total water consumption: 50 gallons (and we still smelled good!)

The jungle islands of the Marquesas Islands are the real-life embodiment of 1,000 movie and story plots—from Melville's *Taipee* to Somerset Maugham's steamy *Miss Thompson* and its various film incarnations, *Rain,* and *Miss Sadie Thompson.* More recently, the film *Rapa Nui* played fast and loose with historical fact while satisfying the purient interests of those of us who misspent our youth thumbing through *National Geographic.* We discovered that the reality of the Marquesas archipelago and culture, the wellspring of Polynesian society, is much more historic and mysterious than the plot of any mere novel. These relatively untouched volcanic remnants drip with tropical ambience, the dark and ancient *tapu* customs of the Polynesian culture, and the natural generosity of an unspoiled people.

We fell in love with the Marquesas, and had no desire to leave. In fact, we left only after being politely but firmly requested to do so a year later by William, a friendly but professional Marquesan gendarme. By the time we left, we had to go north to Hawaii to refit and replenish the cruising kitty. After these islands, for us there was no Bora Bora, no New Zealand, no Cocos Keeling. We didn't need to find those places; the Marquesas had satisfied all our tropical dreams.

# PART ONE:
# INTRODUCING THE MARQUESAS

## The Legend of Creation

The Adam and Eve of the Marquesas were Atua and his wife Atanua. They were the parents of the two chiefs Nuku and Petane of Hiva Oa. Unfortunately, Atua and Atanua had nowhere to live and were forced to fly around over the open sea.

Atanua became tired and asked her husband to build them a home. He was also glad to stop flying around and called upon the spirits of mankind to build a house. At sundown the spirits got busy and started by erecting two (Ua) posts (Pou). Next, they placed between the posts a ridge pole (Hiva) that was long (Oa) enough to span the two posts. Then, the roof poles (Nuku) and supports (Hiva) were added. The roof thatching (Fatu) was made with nine Hiva (pronounced and written "iva" in modern times)—bundles of thatching, each containing 2,000 palmetto leaves. Two (Ua) holes (Huka) were dug to burn the refuse after the structure was completed.

Eiao, Mohotani and Fatu Uku describe the different times and the jobs completed prior to the arrival of the fire (Tahu) spirit (ata) at sunrise. (The Ua Hukans are not particularly fond of being accused of living on an island named for two refuse pits!)

# The Marquesas Islands

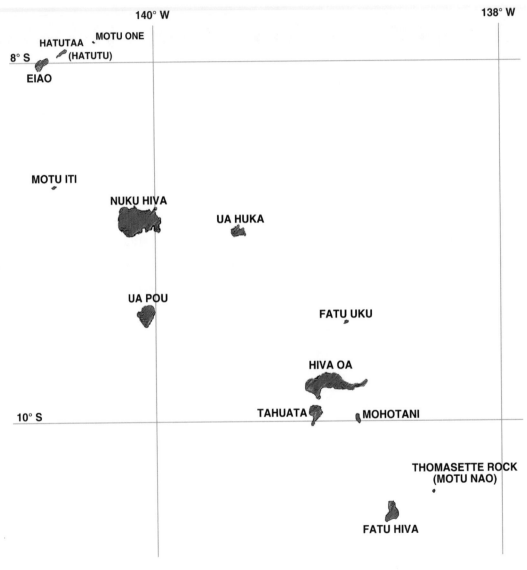

140° W

138° W

HATUTAA · MOTU ONE

8° S ⌁ (HATUTU)

EIAO

MOTU ITI

NUKU HIVA

UA HUKA

UA POU

FATU UKU

HIVA OA

TAHUATA  MOHOTANI

10° S

THOMASETTE ROCK
(MOTU NAO)

FATU HIVA

# Chapter 1

# HISTORY

### Early Migration and Settlement

Marquesan history is filled with by contradictions between archeological evidence and Marquesan oral history. Carbon dating of the excavated remains of cooking fires and, in some cases human bones, places the original migrations of Polynesian people to the Marquesas between 500 and 300 BC. These first settlers came from the southwest Pacific, probably Tonga and Samoa via the Cook Islands. They sailed northeast past the Society Islands and Tahiti, possibly unaware of their existence. They may have found the Tuamotu but those low atolls are arid and agriculturally unproductive, so they probably picked a few coconuts and continued northeastward. They eventually found the Marquesas, settling first on Nuku Hiva or Ua Pou.

One of the most important aspects of Marquesan history is the currently accepted theory that later exploratory voyages by the Marquesans resulted in the settling of what is now Polynesia, including the Tuamotus, Hawaii, the Society Islands (which include Bora Bora, Moorea and Tahiti), New Zealand (via the Cooks) and Easter Island. There is some evidence of a reverse migration back to Tonga and Samoa.

Language may offer a few clues. The Hawaiian language is very close to Marquesan, and with the transposition of a few consonants, the two societies communicate well. However, only about 20% of the Marquesan language corresponds to Tahitian. The difference in language between the Marquesas and the Society Islands is evidence that the two societies developed independently although they were settled at the same time. It is difficult to find any pre-0 AD sites in Tahiti as the island is gradually sinking and most of the older sites are now underwater.

The line between history and myth in the Marquesas is also fuzzy. As late as the 1940s some older Marquesans could still recite their genealogy back to the first two quasi-mythical chiefs, brothers Nuku and Petane, sons of Atea and Atanua, the god/people who "built" the islands; between the two of them, they controlled all of Hiva Oa. The area west of Taahuku was controlled by Nuku and the eastern side to the tip of Matafenua was overseen by Petane. The individual tribes within these two groups were roughly identified by the valleys they inhabited. The tribes on Petane's side of the island were constantly battling each other. However, they would always join forces against their arch foes, the Na'iki, Nuku's people.

The Marquesas Archipelago is divided geographically into a northern group, the main islands of which are Nuku Hiva, Ua Huka and Ua Pou, and a southern group comprised of Hiva Oa, Tahuata and Fatu Hiva. The catch-all name for the tribes on Hiva Oa around Atuona is Na'iki. The Marquesans of the other two southern populated islands, Tahuata and Fatu Hiva, readily admit their colonies sprang from the Na'iki. The people of the Northern group are reticent to admit a genealogical connection with the Na'iki although archeological evidence points to a definite migration of Na'iki to Nuku Hiva, and there is no evidence indicating a southern migration. The oral history of Hiva Oa is doubtful as the preponderance of evidence shows that the first settlers were on Ua Pou or Nuku Hiva.

## The Arrival of the Hao' e

*"Among the islands of Polynesia, no sooner are the images overturned, the temples demolished and the idolaters converted to nominal Christians, than disease, vice, and premature death make their appearance. The depopulated land is recruited from the rapacious hordes of enlightened individuals who settle themselves within its borders and clamorously announce the progress of the truth. Neat villas, trim gardens, shaved lawns, spires and cupolas arise while the poor savage soon finds himself an interloper in the country of his fathers, and that too on the very site of the hut where he was born. The spontaneous fruits of the earth, which God in his wisdom ordained for the support of the indolent natives are remorselessly seized up and appropriated by the stranger, are devoured before the eyes of starving inhabitants or sent on board the numerous vessels which now touch at their shores." — **Herman Melville**

Nowhere in Oceania was Herman's description more appropriate than in the Marquesas. The downhill slide for traditional Marquesan society began in 1595 when an expedition financed by the Viceroy of Peru stumbled on the southern three inhabited islands. Alvaro Mendaña de Neira was the expedition leader and Pedro Fernandez de Quiros, working for the king of Spain, was the pilot. The islands were supposedly named after the wife of the Viceroy—she was the Marquesa de Mendoza. Another story is that the islands were named after the Viceroy himself who was also a marquis. The rather bulky name of the islands then would have been "Las Islas del Marques Don Garcia Hurtado de Mendoza de Canete." Other than the fact the long name sounds stupid, I tend to go with the first version. I figure Mendaña was fooling around with the wife of the Viceroy, but that's my version.

No matter which story is true, the name stuck despite the fact that Mendaña found only the southern group; his visit was the first and last notable Spanish incursion into the Marquesas. He gave Hiva Oa the name of La Dominica; Tahuata was called Santa Christina; Mohotane (Motane), San Pedro and Fatu Hiva was named Magdelena.

Mendaña's only effect on the islands was negative. His marines indiscriminately shot and killed some 200 Marquesans including 70 Tahuatans and it is said that his actions are the reasons why no Europeans live on Tahuata to this day.

So, by now the *hao'e* [hah-oh-eh] or white man, had learned of the southern group. But 200 years passed before the northern group was visited by another gringo. In 1791, American Captain Joseph Ingraham landed aboard a trading vessel, the *Hope,* and named the northern islands. Tiny Hatutaa (Hatutu) was called Hanack, Eiao was called Knox; Nuku Hiva was named Federal. Ua Huka lucked out and got the name Washington. The name Adams was given to Ua Pou where, in Hakahau, there is a plaque commemorating the visit.

Naming these islands seems to be the only interest the expedition leaders had up to that time. The sailors, on the other hand, were intensely interested in the young women who gave of themselves freely. This led to the tragic deaths of thousands of islanders by venereal disease and other illnesses against which the Marquesans had no immunity.

Ingraham claimed the islands in the name of the U.S. and sailed off secure in the knowledge that Federal Island was the newest outpost of the newest republic. Then one month later, Etienne Marchand sailed into the area and claimed the archipelago for France. He named Hatutaa, Chanal; Eiao, Massé. Nuku Hiva was called Beaux and at Ua Pou his imagination gave out and he named it after himself; Ua Huka got the name of his ship, *Le Solide*.

A year later in 1792, British Captain Richard Hergest arrived. Missing Hatutaa altogether, he named Eiao, Robert; Nuku Hiva was called Sir Henry Martin; Ua Huka became Riou, and Ua Pou got the name Trevennen. He then hauled in the main sheet and sailed away.

Next was Roberts, another gringo, who named the islands again. Ua Huka became Massachusetts. (The resemblance is indisputable, particularly the climate.) But in 1813, things got serious as U.S. Navy Commodore David Porter, aboard the frigate *Essex*, established a military base on Nuku Hiva. Taiohae was renamed Madisonville after the president. Although the Commodore petitioned the U.S. Congress to annex the islands it neglected to act and the colony failed. The last American foray into the Marquesas was over.

In 1842, Rear-Admiral Abel Dupetit-Thouars, one of a long line of French Navy commanders, arrived off Tahuata. With a squadron backing him up, the Admiral forced Marquesan chiefs to sign allegiance to King Louis Philippe. He set up garrisons on Tahuata and Nuku Hiva in an attempt to reinforce the authority of France. The forts did not last long as the bases were costly, and the Marquesas were of no significant military or economic value to France.

Military influence had waned; a series of administrators came and went. The greatest change occurred in the middle of the 19th century when the nuns arrived. The appearance of the Catholic and Protestant missionaries had a profound effect on the islands. A two-panel cartoon in a Fiji newspaper was worth 2,000 words about the influence of the church on South Pacific islanders. The first panel showed two 19th century, Bible-toting missionaries pointing disapprovingly at two islanders, one of each sex, dressed only in the traditional loin cloths. The caption read, "Couvrez-vous, sauvages" ("Cover yourselves, savages!"). The second panel showed two modern-day, conservatively dressed islanders, Bibles in hand pointing disapprovingly at two tourists, one of each sex, dressed in dental floss bathing suits. The caption was, of course: "Couvrez-vous, sauvages!"

From the arrival of the missionaries until 1922, the most notable event befalling the Marquesans was massive depopulation. Sickness had been rare among the islanders before the arrival of Europeans. The odd accident, war, murder or sacrifice were the only misfortunes interrupting an otherwise full life. The ancient Marquesans suffered only occasionally from bronchitis, asthma, impetigo, an abscess, leprosy, blindness, deafness, pains to the joints and dementia. When any of these afflictions did manifest themselves, it was considered punishment by a god for trespassing on a *tapu*, a sacred icon, or act, as decided by the Marquesan priests. Leprosy was considered punishment for touching menstrual blood; insanity was caused by eating a tapu fruit; an abscess was reproof for eating a type of fish reserved for the priests. (Medicines, however effective or ineffective they may have been, were considered useless without an accompanying chant; magic was more important than the medicine itself.

When Commodore Porter arrived in 1813, he estimated the total population of the Marquesas at around 80,000 souls. Just 80 years later the population had fallen to 2,094 inhabitants for the Marquesans had no natural immunity to the diseases brought by Europeans. Among the worst killers was smallpox brought unwittingly into the Marquesas by the islanders themselves. In the 1860s a Peruvian "blackbirding" expedition kidnapped 20 Marquesans and hauled them off to Peru to work as slaves in the silver mines. The French who were outraged demanded the return of the men. After several years of slavery they were returned to Nuku Hiva, bringing pneumonia and smallpox. Relatives and friends of the men who visited them returned to the other islands spreading smallpox throughout the archipelago.

In 1923, Dr. Louis Rollin arrived as the chief medical officer for the Marquesas. Appalled by what he saw he moved quickly to decrease the morbidity rate. During that year, in the northern group of 1004 inhabitants, there were 48 births and 52 deaths. One-third of the deaths were infants under a year of age. That was the last year of population decrease. The first several years of Doctor Rollin's tenure as head physician saw rapid improvement in the statistics. The resurrection of the Marquesan population is one accomplishment which the French can point to with pride, and Dr. Rollin was largely responsible. The present population of six inhabited islands is approximately 8,000 souls.

## The Marquesas Today

The current political situation is complex. The Marquesas are a unit of French Polynesia, along with the Tuamotus, the Austral Islands, Gambier and the Society Islands; their capital is Papeete on Tahiti. The Marquesas are allowed two elected representatives to the territorial legislature.

Economic and political power is jealously guarded in Papeete—the only official port of entry. As long as Papeete is the only *official* port of entry for visitors arriving other than by boat, the isolated Marquesas will continue to be a haven for cruise boats.

All but a token amount of the tax income generated in French Polynesia comes from import taxes. Since all imported goods come through Papeete, the distribution system is based there. Virtually nothing is exempt from the taxes that can reach higher than 100%; the cost of shipping is also taxed. The distribution companies in Papeete add their profit, then ship the products to the Marquesas. This concentration of political and economic power is one of the reasons a quart of mayonnaise costs $11 U.S. and a head of cabbage $9 in Taiohae.

The major town on each island has an elected mayor who is the administrative head of the island but who must answer to the chief administrator sent from Tahiti. The minor towns elect a mayor who serves as second, third, or fourth in the chain of command on the island. Taiohae is the capital of the Marquesas and a representative from Papeete and France act as administrators in cooperation with the elected mayors. The Marquesans vote for the president of France and, of course, for the French Polynesian representative to the French National Legislature.

# Chapter 2

# ARCHEOLOGY IN THE MARQUESAS

The Marquesas archipelago is one enormous archeological site; there are ruined stone platforms (*paepae*) everywhere, and archeological materials are likely to turn up almost anywhere you dig. The annotated list below contains the names of high-interest sites, mostly featuring complexes of large stone structures. The buildings and statues on these sites date from AD 1600-1700 at most, since such massive stonework in the Marquesas (or elsewhere in Polynesia) is not ancient. These impressive buildings and feats of civil engineering fall into two principal categories: *tohua*, which are large, rectangular ceremonial plazas, constructed by tribes for public ceremonies; and *me'ae*, which are temples, and often indistinguishable from house platforms (*paepae*).

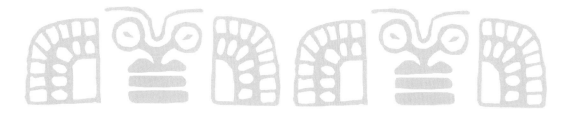

# Annotated List of Notable Sites

(Compiled by Robert Suggs)

## NUKU HIVA

### Taioha'e

**Tohua Kou'eva**    Relatively well-preserved site with unusual petroglpyhs.

**Paepae Pikivehine**    Residence of Queen Vaekehu, last ruler of the Marquesas, stands on a tohua.

### Ha'apa'a

**Vaihi petroglyph site**    On the ridge between Vaihi and Vaituku valleys.

### Taipivai

**Tohua Vahangeku'a** *(Vahakeku'a in modern Taipi dialect)*    The site of the largest house platform in the archipelago. This site was burned by the U.S. Navy under Commodore David Porter in 1813 during a U.S. raid into Taipi.

**Pa'eke**    Believed to be a kind of tribal pantheon, with tiki representing the dieties of the Taipi subtribes. This site was first photographed in 1896.

**Tohua Teiviohou**    Also known as "Melville's pae-pae", traditionally the site where the great American novelist lived during his three-week sojourn among the Taipi, 1843.

### Hatiheu

**Tohua Hikoku'a**    Ceremonial center of the Ati Papua tribe, with a statue of the goddess Tevanau'au'a built into the wall of a platform at the seaside-end of the dance floor and several rather elaborate modern statues.

**Tohua Kamuihei**    Recently restored by the French archeologist, Pierre Ottino, has an extensive petroglyph gallery associated with it.

**Me'ae Te i'i poka**    Also sacred to the goddess Tevanaua'ua'a, famous for its mysterious atmosphere, and as the site of one of the last human sacrifices in the 19th century. A Ha'apa'a tribesman, supposedly travelling under safe conduct, was lured to his death here.

.

**Ha'atuatua**  An open beach dune site of the late BC era. Although very little of archeological interest is visible on the surface, this is one of the most beautiful beaches in the archipelago.

> **WARNING!**  The beach is infested with blood-sucking flies and the beautiful surf hides dangerous undertows as well as large marine life.

## UA HUKA
### Hane

**Me'ae Me'aieaute**  A temple of the Tititea tribe, has a number of small tiki, including a much damaged copy of the statue of the pregnant goddess found at Te I'i pona in Puama'u, Hiva Oa (see below).

The beach dune at Hane conceals a deep open village site which dates back to the last centuries BC, according to Prof. Pat Kirch, of the University of California, Berkeley.

## UA POU
### Hakamoui

**Me'ae Menaha Taka'oa**  The most sacred site on the island, was dedicated to the memory of the Atua Heato, a chief who lived during the early 1800s and upon his death was elevated to the status of a god. Heato, who was said to have enormous supernatural powers, was unusual in that he was not tattooed. The remains of Heato and his nephew Taiuao (who succeeded him as chief) were buried at this site.

## TAHUATA
### Vaitahu

Archeological exhibit in the Chief's office from excavations conducted by Prof. Rolett (University of Hawai'i) at Hanamiai.

### Hapatoni

**Me'ae Mahi'a**  A temple of the Taiuoho tribe, recently restored by the French archeologist, Pierre Ottino.

## FATU HIVA

Stone architecture on this island was less well-developed; while ruins are everywhere, the rest of the archipelago has no sites comparable to those listed above. Isolated petroglyphs may be found in both Hanavave and O'omoa. There is a very good museum in O'omoa, near the chapel.

## HIVA OA
### Tahauku

*Tohua* and associated petroglpyh site in Teueto valley.

### Ta'a'oa

A huge ceremonial complex of the Tiu tribe, the largest of its type in the Marquesas. The site consists of a large Nuku Hiva style tohua and many terraces, temple with sacred banyans, and mortuary platforms, extending up the hill from the tohua. The site is presided over by Iupeke, a large tiki carved in low relief on a basalt column near the upper end of the site.

### Puama'u

**Me'ae Te i'i pona**   Large stone tiki standing on a well-restored ceremonial site of the Na'iki tribe. The most interesting statues on this site are those of Taka'i'i, the largest stone statue west of Easter Island, and Maki'i tau 'a pepe, a statue with a box-like protuberance on its stomach. This is the statue of the priestess Tau'a Pepe, who died giving birth to a male child (who survived). The statue, carved by her husband, shows her in the throes of death (maki'i). The several large stone heads scattered around the site commemorate human victims offered to the gods here.

Tiki at Puama'u

# Chapter 3

# THE NATURAL ENVIRONMENT

# Geology

With the exception of tiny Motu One (Sand Cay), all the islands of the Marquesas are volcanic in origin. Basaltic cones, cliffs and spires are the trademarks of the Marquesas. The structures of dark rock that form forbidding Gothic castles on vertical walls are aptly described as "King Kong's Islands." The fantastic spires of Ua Pou were formed by subterranean magma hardening as it was pushed slowly above the surface. This phenomenon occurred also on Martinique in the Caribbean, but there the spires fell over instead of standing majestically above the anchorages as at Hakahau and Hakahetau.

The archipelago was formed in a northwest-to-southeast direction. The ancient volcano crater of Taaoa on Hiva Oa is the exception to the rule, starting its island-forming eruptions 6.5 million years ago. Before Taaoa was completely formed, Eiao in the northwest began its growth followed by Nuku Hiva, Ua Pou, Ua Huka, and Tahuata. Then, the Puamau Volcano formed the eastern part of Hiva Oa and finally Fatu Hiva was built about 1.42 to 1.30 million years ago. This pattern represents volcanic activity moving southeast along the East Pacific Ridge at the blinding speed of 9.9 centimeters per year.

The unusual lack of coral reefs in the Marquesas which normally guard the entrances to tropical anchorages is explained by several theories. The most reasonable one attributes periodic seawater temperature changes to "El Niño." (It is interesting to note that the oft reproached "El Niño" current was identified and named prior to 1930. Its name, The Child, is a reference to the Christ Child, as the phenomenon is usually recognized around Christmas time and is said to occur in periods of minimum sun spot activity). The failure of the Peruvian Current to follow its normal course allows this smaller current, "El Niño," to spread its higher temperatures throughout the western Pacific. This slight increase in temperature may be the reason for the scarcity of large coral formations.

The coral that does exist generally grows deeper in the bays where it is protected from pelagic currents. There are beautiful coral beds on the west and north coast of Tahuata. Hapatoni and Hana Tefau also have sizable colonies. The bays north of Vaitahu have white sand beaches formed by the disintegration of coral colonies. Hanaiapa on the north shore of Hiva Oa is coral-lined but is a little deep for convenient snorkeling. The reef most similar to Caribbean coral formations is located at Anaho on the northeast side of Nuku Hiva. Coral is "puka" in Marquesan (it also means limestone) and the description of Anaho in Part 2 will give you a better idea of the marvelous "puka" reef found there.

Cliffs at Taioa Bay, Nuku Hiva

# Fauna

There are only a few animals of importance on the Marquesas and most were introduced by man. The Marquesans brought pigs when they migrated to and from the other Pacific Islands. The feral pigs are firmly established as a target for hunters who, with a few farmers, supply this staple food for the islanders.

Goats were introduced to the islands by Captain Cook who stopped at Vaitahu on Tahuata in 1774. They are deliciously prepared in a number of ways. (See Appendix D for recipe). But the supply exceeds the demand and goats are a pest on some islands and have contributed to significant defoliation and the resulting erosion.

Horses were introduced by French Admiral Dupetit Thuars and today the small Marquesan ponies can be seen carrying hunters through the brush of the highlands. On special holidays they are used for racing and they are exercised on the beach at Taiohae every day. Most islands have wild horses free for the taking. . . if you can catch them.

Cats are ubiquitous and wild ones abound. The island dogs have adapted well to the islands, but no one knows their origin. Invariably gentle toward humans, they are fierce hunters. The Marquesans do not treat their pets as members of the family as we do, and dogs and cats are generally not allowed inside homes. The Marquesans have adapted an English phrase to tell a dog to leave. They yell, "Keerow!" which is how their ears interpret "Get out!" Shipboard pets are not legally allowed on shore although I suspect that some cruising boats take their dogs into the less-inhabited bays. The authorities are rightfully worried about the spread of disease, so it's best to leave your pets on board.

There are a couple of bird species unique to the Marquesas, one of which was found on Ua Huka only recently—the Marquesan Larakeet, a pretty green-and-blue relative of the parrot. In 1994, representatives of the San Diego Zoo traveled to Ua Huka to find nests of this rare bird and redistributed a clutch or two to Hiva Oa. Another unique species, the Upe, which is found only on Nuku Hiva looks like a big pigeon. There are just 100 or so remaining.

Wild chickens abound. Marquesans have overbred them to the point where many returned to the jungle and reverted to their original state.

Every day pairs of a beautiful white bird called Pitake (Topic Bird) dive and wheel in unison over the anchorages of Fenua Enata. These birds resemble small, white dog-fighting sport kites and are especially active over Taiohae Bay.

Marquesan horses
on the beach

# Insects

There are a few insects of particular interest to the visitor. The most infamous is the evil NoNo—an almost-invisible biting bug that comes in two varieties. The White NoNo lives on the beach and its cousin, the Black NoNo, lives inland. They disappear at night so after sundown you are safe from their attacks. However, with simple precautions, the NoNo problem can be alleviated by a lot of insect repellant and *more* insect repellant. If you run out of insect repellant, buy some monoi oil and spread it on liberally. (Monoi oil is coconut oil normally scented with tiare, sandlewood or vanilla which drowns the NoNos before they bite.) Lime juice is also a good repellant.

With time, some people gain a degree of immunity against the saliva of the NoNo and the bites become less bothersome. Yours truly is immune and has never suffered from NoNos. Observers have wrongly attributed my good fortune to an inordinately high percentage of Hinano beer in the bloodstream. Though it is common knowledge that they

Lizard tatoo motif

bite only at night, a friend took a nap next to our campfire on the beach at Hana Moe Noa one evening. The next day he found himself covered in insect bites which he swore were NoNo bites, but I think they were caused by mosquitos. Perhaps the jury is still out on the nocturnal activities of the NoNo.

The reputation of the NoNo precedes itself. In May of 1995, Hawaiians reenacted the historic voyages of discovery by ancient Polynesians. After an arduous return journey from Nuku Hiva, the Hawaiian canoes were held offshore of the big island of Hawaii while the Coast Guard dropped canisters of insecticide into the canoes. It seems the NoNos had hitched a ride and their presence threatened the tourist industry in the State of Hawaii.

Although mosquitoes are present in the Marquesas, they don't seem to be as big a problem as they are on most tropical islands. People tend to blame the NoNos for bites after sundown but it's usually a wayward mosquito. Again, insect repellant is the answer. I have been reminded, however, that the effects of a NoNo bite often do not appear until some hours after the bite.

Fire ants exist on the islands but their danger and discomfort are not enough to warrant a discussion here.

Centipedes are a different story. Before you pick up dry rocks, dead stumps, cardboard boxes or anything else that could hide this ugly insect, move the object with a stick first. Anything that lies around for a long time is an attractive home for a centipede. Their bite is painful and can be dangerous to sensitive people. The centipede is distinct from the millipede, which is round, harmless and slow moving. The centipede is a flat, articulated, fast-moving insect. It moves like a snake and grows to as long as 10 inches with ugly, venomous pincers at the rear. Ugh!

# Flora

This brief list of the major decorative and edible plants you find in the Marquesas does not even scratch the surface of plant life thriving on the islands but it is a representative sample.

**Acacia** - *Acacia Farnesiana* is a scourge. Growing 20 to 50 feet, this plant which was originally imported to decorate a cemetery has taken over most valleys of the islands. For some reason, even the overpopulation of goats and pigs cannot faze this blight.

**Banana** *(meika)* - There are many varieties of banana. Some are used for cooking and some of the smaller varieties are as sweet as anything you have ever tasted.

**Bougainvillea** - The "electric" colors of this tropical vine are not produced by its almost invisible flowers but rather by leaves and bracts surrounding them. The most dramatic ones I saw are the psychedelic double lavender vines in front of the Catholic church at Hakahetau on Ua Pou.

**Breadfruit** *(tumu mei)*- *Arcotocarpus Alticis*, this scourge of Captain Bly and the mutinous crew of the *Bounty*, has been a staple on the Marquesan archipelago since ancient times. The fruit is called *me'i* and when fermented it is called *ma;* mixed with fresh *me'i* or tapioca (manioc) it gives the ubiquitous but glutenous popoi. The breadfruit tree grows to great heights; the ripe fruit is the size of a bowling ball, and the dark green leaves are over a foot long and deeply pennate. The fruit can be cooked like a potato but it is normally just tossed directly on the coals of a fire being used to cook a pig or goat.

**Coconut** *(tumu ehi)* - You have probably heard of a coconut tree before so I will not burden you with a long botanical description. However, I feel compelled to wax poetic on the culinary advantages to cooking with coconut milk. My "World Famous Poisson Cru Recipe" (see the Appendix for the recipe) has a complete explanation of the process for making coconut milk. If you need a live demonstration of how to shuck and shred a coconut, I recommend asking Leo or André at Anaho. Also, you can buy a *rapacoco* (coconut grater) at most of the *magasins* (stores) in the main villages. This little tool makes quick work of shredding coconut meat and readies it for juicing. A *rapacoco* costs about $11 and is well worth the investment. (Notice I have omitted any mention of health benefits of coconut-derived foods. There aren't many.)

**Frangipani** - *Plumeria Rubra* is the tropical dream tree; its scent is the inspiration of poets. Its windmill flowers range in color from white to cream and red. The trees, growing rarely over 12 feet, have few leaves but the blooms are marvelous. Death is associated with the Frangipani and the Marquesans use them in funerals.

**Gardenia** *(tiare)* - *Gardenia Tahitiensis*, the official flower of Tahiti, grows prolifically in the Marquesas. The round shrub has shiny ovate green leaves and grows to about 10 feet. The flower is about an inch in diameter, beautifully

Breadfruit

scented and can often be seen worn behind the ear of both men and women. The men usually wear the unopened bud while women wear the flower opened behind either the right or left ear. I have wasted a significant amount of time researching the significance of a flower placed behind the right ear versus a blossom placed behind the left ear to no avail.

**Hibiscus** *(ko'ute)- Rosa Sinensis*. This shrub with dark green leaves produces large flowers in every color of the rainbow. The double reds are as spectacular on the plant as they are over the ears of the Marquesan women. Hawaii claims the hybiscus as its state flower.

**Ironwood** *(toa)- Casuarina Equisetifolia*, the "Horsetail Tree" or Australian Pine was used for making heavy *cassetêtes* and other weapons in ancient times. The Keikahanui Inn at Taiohae on Nuku Hiva has several large specimens on its property. On the beach near the water spigot at Anaho a clothesline is attached to a line of 5 or 6 ironwoods. The Ironwood is so heavy that it does not float. The *cassetêtes* carved today are made of lighter *to'u* or rosewood.

**Mango** - *Mangifera indica*, one of the 20 to 30 different cultivars thriving in Fenua Enata. The biggest tree I've seen is at Magasin Kamake near the "Y" in the road. After 3 p.m., this monster tree is usually filled with kids picking a free, after-school snack.

**Sensitive Plant** - *Mimosa pudica*- Pantropic, "Live and Die,"or "Touch Me Not." Remarkable because its leaflets close and the petioles drop at the slightest touch. It is one of the few plants having stickers that will hurt your feet as you pad around the islands. Its small florescent-pink flower hugs the ground. Its appearance is darker green than surrounding weeds and grass and, with practice, you will learn to side-step this guy. It is found on all the islands.

**Tapioca Plant** *(manioc)* - Manihot Esculenta or Cassava. The starchy tubers are dried and ground into flour and used as an additive to fermented breadfruit to make popoi.

## Citrus Fruit

The ubiquitous lime is the secret to Marquesan cooking and many fishermen carry a handful of limes with them when fishing to use as a portable oven. *Poisson cru* (literally translated as "raw fish") is a staple in the islands. (See the aforementioned *poisson cru recipe*" in the Appendix where I also have included the instructions for preserving lime juice.)

The other common citrus fruit in the Marquesas is the Tahitian pamplemousse (grapefruit). The grapefruit in these islands seem to suffer from a thyroid problem. They are huge! The flesh is green and the sweetest I ever tasted. They never need sugar and they have a unique, delicious flavor.

Ua Huka is the citrus capital of the islands; oranges from Ua Huka are shipped to all the other islands of the group.

# Chapter 4

# ARRIVING IN THE MARQUESAS

### Getting there

Briefly, there are three main routes that cruising vessels seem to take. The closest one—and the best in my view—is to leave from the West Coast of the U.S. and cruise non-stop to the Marquesas. This is the nearest of the jump-off points, for as you travel southeast along the North American continent, you draw farther and farther away from the Marquesas. The other two traditional routes—from Panama or Central America—add at least 1,000 miles to your itinerary.

The most annoying part of a trip from Panama or the Galapagos to the Marquesas is the effect of the Intertropical Convergence Zone (ITCZ). This meandering, windless but sometimes wet band of tropical humidity which wanders just north or south of the equator separates the Northeast trades and the Southeast trades. This lack of wind makes 45- to 60-day voyages from Panama and the Galapagos not uncommon.

# Ports of Entry

Let's assume you have already managed to get yourself to the Marquesas. Here are some tips and suggestions.

The only official ports of entry to French Polynesia are in the Society Islands; the Marquesas are not an official port of entry. However, as a courtesy, the government does allow yachts to check in at the Marquesas which solves a multitude of problems for cruisings boaters. As mentioned earlier, all goods must enter through Papeete, Tahiti where they are taxed, warehoused, and shipped before reaching the Marquesas, making the prices for imported goods prohibitively expensive. Also, tourism in the archipelago is very limited because all airline passengers must enter through Papeete before flying on to the Marquesas. The airline fare from Papeete to Nuku Hiva (3 hours) is more expensive than an easily available bargain fare between Los Angeles and Tahiti (8 hours), and the tourist industry in Papeete intends to keep it that way.

I suggest that you make your first landfall at Atuona, Taahuku Bay on Hiva to ensure that most of your cruising is done with fair winds. (If you start at either of the other two legal check-in points—Taiohae on Nuku Hiva or Hakahau on Ua Pou—a tour of the islands could include some uncomfortable beating to weather which we all know, is unacceptable.

# Navigating through Customs

No matter which of the three islands you chose for your first landfall, entry procedures are the same. The captain and crew should arrive at the gendarmerie with passports in hand. The captain should have an inventory of the vessel's equipment which will be an addendum to the ship's "passport" issued by the gendarme. This passport must be presented *every* time you enter an anchorage in French Polynesia where there is an official gendarmerie. (There are only three such islands in the Marquesas.) Every time you

travel to Taiohae on Nuku Hiva, Hakahau on Ua Pou or Atuona, on Hiva Oa, you must present your boat's "passport" to be stamped. You don't have to be silly about it though. If you checked in at Taiohae and left to spend a weekend in Anaho, you do not have to check back in at Taiohae upon your return. Check in *only* if the last stamp in the "passport" is different from your new anchorage.

If you happen to be one of the few boats spot checked by customs (*douane*), they will compare your equipment list with the physical inventory of your vessel. If you possess items not included on your list, they will presume you brought them to sell and will tax you on the spot. If there are items on the list but not on your boat, they will presume you have sold them and tax you on the spot. Either way you lose, so make out your inventory list *accurately* as the visits of the *douane* boat are on the increase.

U.S. citizens are allowed 30 days in French Polynesia without a visa. After that time, you must pay a fee to stick around. The visa, available at the post office, costs about U.S. $10.00 per month for a three-month increment.

Gendarmerie at Taiohae, Nuku Hiva

# Bond

Each crew member is required to post a bond with Banque Socredo in an amount equal to the price of economy class air fare from Papeete to the nearest port of entry of the crew member's home country. For Americans, this ranges from $750 to $1,200 U.S. depending on who's working the counter at Socredo the day you apply. For French citizens it is worse. One family of six arrived to receive the bad news they would have to fork over the equivalent of $12,000 U.S. for their bond. ($2,000 a head). This bond is refunded to you when you check out of French Polynesia. However, here's the catch—the bank will withhold a fee *and* an exchange rate fee so you lose a few percentage points in the transaction.

But here's some good news. In 1998, the gendarmerie was still allowing yachts to enter the Marquesas without paying the bond. They take it for granted you will continue on to Papeete where you will finally pay up. This is just a courtesy for visiting boats which can be rescinded at any time.

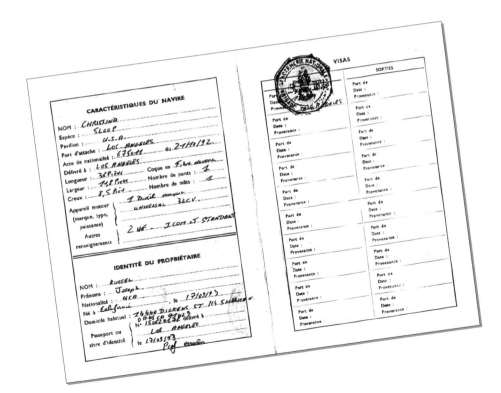

## People of the Marquesas Islands

# PART TWO:
# NAVIGATION AND ANCHORAGES

## The Legend of the NoNo Flies

The father of a powerful chief on Nuku Hiva died. The chief needed to build a large *paepae* to hold the body of his deceased father. It had to be built of large rocks but there were no such rocks to be had on Nuku Hiva. A chieftess on Hiva Oa lived in an area with plenty of the rocks that would fit the bill. The chieftess told the Nuku Hiva chief that if he would transport the chieftess and her husband to Nuku Hiva from Hiva Oa, she would give him all the stones needed for a paepae befitting a king.

The Nuku Hiva chief agreed and traveled to Hiva Oa in a huge pirogue. The vessel was loaded with huge stones and the chieftess and her entourage came aboard. Everything went hunky-dory until the canoe neared Nuku Hiva half way between Taiohae and Ua Pou. Here, the grieving chief realized the stones were tapu for women. They were not allowed to come near them, much less accompany them on such a voyage.

The chieftess and her husband were thrown overboard. The chieftess had suspected this treachery and had brought live NoNos buzzing about in clay jars. Just before she went down for the third time, she broke the jars and the NoNos flew to Nuku Hiva and Ua Pou. These two islands never had NoNos until that day. It's a true story, ask anybody.

A long-time friend and author, the late Fritz Seyfarth, to whom this book is dedicated, once guided me through a tricky reef into a relatively unknown but idyllic anchorage in the British Virgin Islands. However, before he would show me the passage through "Killer Reef" he made me promise not to reveal the passage to a certain well-known personnage among Caribbean cruising guide writers. It seems this gentleman has a standing offer: he will foot a rum for anyone who tells him about a new anchorage in the Caribbean. Thanks a lot. As soon as his crummy rum and coke has hit the lips, your new pristine anchorage shows up in his latest Caribbean cruising guide. So the next time you arrive at "Paradise Cove" behind "Killer Reef," the gunkhole will be chock-a-block with white and blue charterboats sporting topless maidens sunning on the foredeck...Hey Fritz – Maybe that guy has the right idea!

Fritz Seyfarth

Cruisers go native

Taahuku Bay, Hiva Oa

# Chapter 5
# HIVA OA

Hiva Oa is one of the islands discovered and named by Mendaña in 1595. He named the island La Dominica. The main town, Atuona, on the southern shore is within Traitors Bay (Taaoa). Whether you arrive from Matafenua, the western tip of Hiva Oa, or up through Bordelais Channel between Tahuata and Hiva Oa, the approach is easy and there are no obstructions.

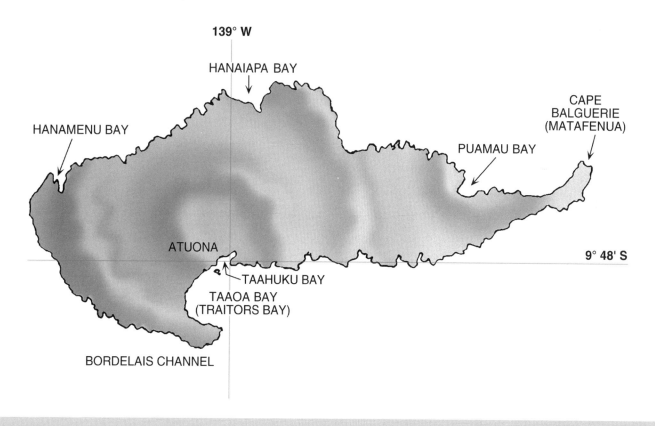

139° W

HANAIAPA BAY

HANAMENU BAY

CAPE BALGUERIE (MATAFENUA)

PUAMAU BAY

ATUONA

9° 48' S

TAAHUKU BAY

TAAOA BAY (TRAITORS BAY)

BORDELAIS CHANNEL

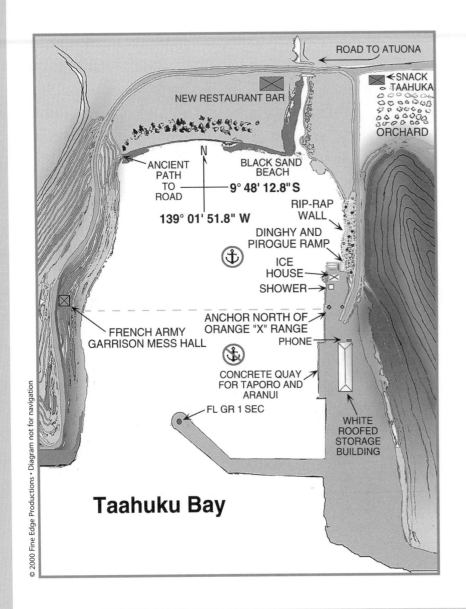

ROAD TO ATUONA

←SNACK TAAHUKA

NEW RESTAURANT BAR

ORCHARD

N

ANCIENT PATH TO ROAD

BLACK SAND BEACH

**9° 48' 12.8" S**

**139° 01' 51.8" W**

RIP-RAP WALL

DINGHY AND PIROGUE RAMP

ICE HOUSE

SHOWER→

ANCHOR NORTH OF ORANGE "X" RANGE

FRENCH ARMY GARRISON MESS HALL

PHONE

CONCRETE QUAY FOR TAPORO AND ARANUI

FL GR 1 SEC

WHITE ROOFED STORAGE BUILDING

**Taahuku Bay**

© 2000 Fine Edge Productions · Diagram not for navigation

# TAAHUKU BAY

## ⚓ ANCHORING TIPS

There is a one-second green flashing light at the end of the stone breakwater. The standard for this light is visible for some distance. *Remember* the buoy colors here are reversed to "green right returning"—the opposite of the U.S.

Once past the breakwater, look for two orange X's on standards on the eastern shore. You must anchor north of the range created by these two X's. (If you anchor south of the range you may be in for a surprise in the middle of the night if the cargo boats *Aranui* or *Taporo* arrive.)

Taahuku is rolly so be prepared to throw out a stern anchor and head 220° magnetic. Anchor in 1 ½ to 3 fathoms of sandy mud, with good holding. The wind sometimes reverses and comes whistling down Taahuku Valley so be sure your stern anchor is secure.

## 🏃 GOING ASHORE

The eastern shore of the bay has a concrete quay, a light-green freezer house and the shower. The best place to land your dinghy is at the pirogue ramp. You cannot see the ramp from the anchorage but just row around the rip-rap wall to the east and you will see it. It's a rocky ramp so your dinghy wheels will only be of limited use. Pull the dinghy well above the ramp so the pirogues can launch. Although the obvious place to tie your dinghy is at the steps in front of the freezer house, the steps are slippery and dangerous, and this could work only if you are careful and set a stern anchor for your dinghy.

# Walking Tour: Atuona

The shower by the freezer house is one of the best in the Marquesas, and the "sink" built into the north side of the shower is great for doing laundry and filling water jugs. In the past, the water has been excellent, but always check with a local to make sure there has been no degradation in quality.

Garbage cans are behind the freezer house and telephones are on the north end of the quay buildings. Fuel and propane can be obtained by calling **Location David**, the car rental place in Atuona; telephone 927-287.

Start your tour of Atuona by walking north up the road. You can usually hitch a ride even if you don't stick out a thumb. If you decide to hoof it, you can have a cold Hinano beer at **Snack Taahuku** about a mile up by the bridge where, by the way, there's a nice swimming hole. Crossing the bridge and continuing up the hill, you arrive at the French army garrison. Along the way there are good spots to take a photo of your boat at anchor. (The best food in town is said to be the army mess hall on the bay side of the road but unfortunately it is closed to the public.)

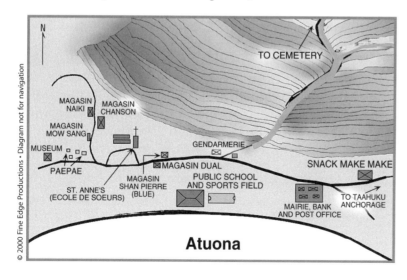

After a hike of a mile or so, you come to the Atuona sign; a few hundred yards beyond it is **Snack Make-Make** *(mah-keh-mah-keh)*. Dani is the owner and Lyn is usually helping out. The food is excellent and the prices are some of the best in the islands. A big juicy hamburger, sometimes on the "specials" list, is good by any standard. The beer is cold and the company pleasant.

Now that you have had your cheeseburger in paradise, it's time to get those letters posted. The post office, bank and town hall are all in the same complex a hundred yards past Make-Make on the opposite side of the street. This complex is called the *mairie* and every major town has one. Calls back home can be placed from here as the postal service is also the telephone company. Don't be surprised if you see the same individuals working at the post office on different islands. The islands exchange postal employees every so often to cover for vacationing workers.

Continue walking west. At the confluence of the main road and the road up to the cemetery there is a small memorial to the two Hiva Oans that died in the World Wars. Adjacent to the memorial is the Gendarmerie and while you are there, check yourselves and your boat into Hiva Oa.

After the simple and pleasant check-in procedure, walk west to one of the oldest buildings on Hiva Oa. The light-blue, two-story market is called **Magasin Shan Pierre**. French Impressionist artist Paul Gauguin, who lived in Atuona during the 19th century, died owing money for wine he bought there. A clock hanging in the corner has 1870 written on it. The remnants of a wire teller's cage reveal that the shop used to house the post office and bank. Merchandise is limited at Magasin Shan Pierre but the beer is cold and, surprisingly, there is a well-stocked stationery department at the back.

The mairie (town hall) in Atuona.

Across from Shan Pierre and fifty yards west is **Magasin Dual**. Here you can find hardware, fishing equipment, t-shirts, and dry goods. The lady in the dry goods section is very friendly and an expert seamstress.

Continuing on, before you reach the bend in the road, the gravel driveway on the right leads to St. Anne's School and church. Nuns first arrived in the Marquesas at Vaitahu on Tahuata in 1847 but returned to France a year later due to a war between tribes on Tahuata and Hiva Oa. They tried to start a congregation and school again on Nuku Hiva in 1864, but then in 1884 the sisters moved to Atuona on Hiva Oa and started St. Anne's School. The school is also known as the *Ecole de Soeur* (the Sister's School) but the Marquesans still call it *Papua Virikine* ("virgin enclosure" in Marquesan) because of Paul Gauguin, whose life in the Marquesas was closely entwined with the school. (See sidebar.)

Once you reach the right bend in the road, you have two choices: visit the **Atuona Museum** or check out the other three grocery stores. If you choose the museum, continue straight past the *paepae* (stone platform) and thatched buildings on the right. These are the grounds for the July fête and other cultural events. The museum is the last building in the complex on the right. Admission is 400 Centîme Franc Pacifique (CFP)(about $4.00 U.S.).

Backtracking to the road, turn left. The first *magasin*, **Mow Sang**—the smallest of the three clustered here—is a bakery where fresh bread is available. Baguettes, price-controlled in French Polynesia, cost about 40 cents a loaf.

Across the road and up the street a few yards is the largest and most complete market, **Magasin Chanson**, which even has a turnstile, bakery, and they accept credit cards. The kid who works at Chanson will take you back to Taahuku in the store's truck if you buy too much to schlep back. (He is the son of my friend Ozanne Rohi, a prominent fisherman on Hiva Oa.)

Next door to Chanson is **Location David**, a car rental operation that can also supply you with diesel. The last *magasin*, **Na'iki**, owned by the mayor, is quite well stocked, but it is not as big as Chanson.

This concludes the easy part of the tour. To take the hike up to Gauguin's grave, backtrack to the gendarmerie and head up the hill at the cross street. In a mile or so you'll see a sign directing you up a road to the left to the *cimetière*. When you arrive at the cemetery, you'll spot Jacques Brel's grave—the first one on the lowest tier under a tree. Gauguin's grave is easier to spot, two tiers up-slope.

## BORDELAIS CHANNEL

If you are westbound, Bordelais Channel, the narrow channel between Hiva Oa and Tahuata, is fun. Southbound, crossing Taaoa Bay from Taahuku is a piece of cake. A gentle breeze normally allows for a broad or beam reach on a port tack. But once you round the point stand by. The wind will begin to pipe within a mile of leaving Taaoa. Before you turn right and head west, it may be a good idea to reduce sail no matter how benign the wind seems at the moment. As the channel narrows, a Venturi effect increases the wind speed until, at the narrowest point, it fairly howls. The wind, along with a smart current, had our full-keel sailboat doing 9 knots over the bottom—and this in a boat that has never seen 10 knots on the taff log.

In closing, I don't recommend sailing east through Bordelais Channel. I did it once and regretted every moment of it.

## Paul Gauguin

Paul Gauguin, the French Impressonist artist, moved to Tahiti in the early part of the 1890s. His reasons for going there varied. First, his paintings were not selling in France and the critics disapproved of his artistic style; second, his sexual proclivities were becoming public knowledge and his supply of 13-year-old French girls was starting to dry up. He lasted several years in Tahiti but was constantly battling the law and the Church. His desire to live the life of a savage was thwarted by the powers-that-be in Tahiti, so he went back to France for a couple of years.

When Gauguin returned to Tahiti his problems were exacerbated by the fact he continued to blast the clergy in editorials he wrote as editor of the local paper. He blamed the unreasonable criticism of the Church for his inability to make a living as an artist. Tehaamana, the 13-year-old girl he fell in love with during his first stay in Tahiti, had since married and he became despondent. Leaving his latest mistress and an illegitimate son behind to fend for themselves, he boarded a copra steamer and arrived in Atuona in early 1901.

Most of the land in and around Atuona then, as now, belonged to the Catholic Church. Gauguin behaved himself long enough to gain the Church's approval to build a house near the store that supplied him with the wine he used to soften up the young girls he courted and seduced. (Though his house has long since disappeared, the old shop, painted light-blue, is still open and called Magasin Shan Pierre.

Once ensconced in his new house, Gauguin reverted to his old ways. He prominently displayed a set of pornographic pictures and a plaque over the door proclaiming the house as "Maison du Jouir." [House of Pleasure]. (Back in Paris between trips, he mounted a plaque in his home engraved, *Te Faruru*, a misspelling of *Te Faaruru*, Tahitian for sexual intercourse which literally means "to cause to shake".) The priests and nuns who were outraged finally found a way to keep the 12- and 13-year-old girls out of his grasp. The Church was the law in those days and the priest simply made attendance at St. Anne's boarding school mandatory for all girls living within a 2 1/2 -mile radius of the campus. This worked for awhile, but Gauguin soon retaliated against the clergy by publicly humiliating them at every opportunity. He sculpted a pornographic statue of the local Bishop and displayed it in his front yard, and he even had the priest's maid as a mistress for a while.

He finally overcame the 2 1/2 -mile attendance law by finding Vaeoho, a 14-year-old girl who lived outside the area. He gave her parents a sewing machine in exchange for their permission to live with her.

But all good things must end and Gauguin was found dead on May 8th, 1903, lying on his bed, surrounded by empty wine bottles and drug ampules. He died fighting the establishment, alcohol, drugs and his own talent.

Gauguin's grave in Atuona is marked by a statue called Oviri (Tahitian for savage) which he sculpted in France between his two Polynesian voyages. Gauguin aspired to "savagehood" in his life and painting, but society was ill-prepared to accept either his lifestyle or his art until well after his death. It is ironic that a man as perverted and disdained in life as Paul Gauguin found artistic renown in death. The Gauguin museum in Papeete is a wellspring of tourist dollars for Tahiti.

# HANAMENU BAY

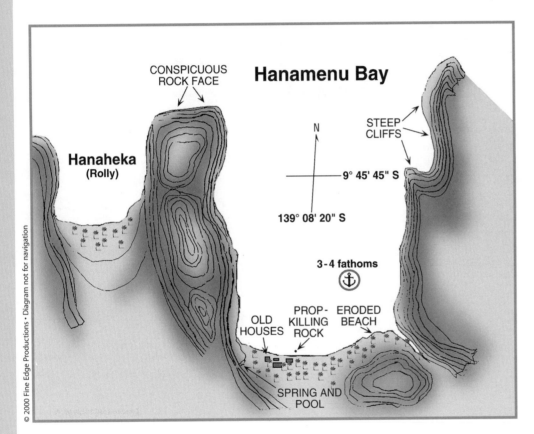

Hanameka
(Rolly)

CONSPICUOUS
ROCK FACE

Hanamenu Bay

N

STEEP
CLIFFS

9° 45' 45" S

139° 08' 20" S

3 - 4 fathoms
⚓

OLD
HOUSES

PROP-
KILLING
ROCK

ERODED
BEACH

SPRING AND
POOL

© 2000 Fine Edge Productions · Diagram not for navigation

## ⚓ ANCHORING TIPS

Hanamenu Bay, on northwestern Hiva Oa, has a straight-forward entrance without hazards. Anchoring in Hanamenu here is like anchoring in the bottom of the Grand Canyon (in miniature) replete with buttes, valleys and terraced cliffs.

**NOTE:** The adjacent bay of Hanaheka is inviting but since it is not as deeply set in as Hanamenu, it can be rolly. Although I have motored through Hanaheka, I have not anchored there. In settled weather it can be as nice as Hanamenu. Try it and send me a report.

Anchoring with only a single bow anchor is fine in 3 to 6 fathoms of sand. If there is no breeze to hold the bow toward shore, you may end up sideways to the swell, so toss a stern anchor out. Anchor left of center to keep away from any rogue swell that might slide around the eastern point. The western cliff making up the point that separates Hanaheka from Hanamenu is shown on the chart as 735 feet high but I doubt it. (Someone might want to pull out that rusty old sextant and give me the exact elevation; I think it's about 300 feet high.)

## 🏃 GOING ASHORE

It is best to land your dinghy at either corner of the beach where the swells are tamer. Also, lurking in the surf 50 yards to the left of the houses, there is a prop-killing rock which you may not see at high tide; it's nearly on the beach and clearly visible at low tide.

# Hanamenu Village Site

When you arrive at Hanamenu, you have left the tropics and traveled to a desert. As Nuku Hiva has *Terre Dessert* (desert land) on the west end, so does Hiva Oa. No one lives at Hanamenu now though there are still houses standing. There are no services or garbage facilities here. If you pack it in, pack it out!

I am tempted to omit this next tidbit because it is special and fragile. Walk behind the *ha'e* (houses) and keep your ears open for water gurgling out of the western hillside. Follow your ears to a most beautiful oasis. In the middle of this palm dessert, Mother Nature (with help from Ozanne Rohi and family) has created a spring that cascades down the cliff side into a pool, 30 foot in diameter, surrounded by breadfruit, multicolored hibiscus, banana trees, ferns and other tropical foliage. The pool is nearly waist deep and is perfect for bathing. There is normally a bar of soap on a flat rock by the pool that belonged to a recently departed and now squeaky clean cruiser. The water is pure and icy cold. Disney could not have built a better scene.

Ozanne, who helped beautify the pool, lived in Hanamenu as a boy. He was shown how to find ancient Marquesan artifacts by visiting archeologists from the Bishop Museum in Hawaii, and his collection of ancient fishhooks, bone and stone implements is highly valued. Ozanne planted a small breadfruit tree (*tumu mei*) behind the middle house, and since the tree doesn't get a lot of water, when you go ashore take along a bucket and dip some water out of the pool to give it a drink.

## The Simple Kindness of the Marquesans

One late afternoon in Hanaiapa, a swimmer approached the *Christina*. Over 60 years old, he looked more like a drowning victim than a swimmer, but he managed to hoist himself up on our inflatable tied to the stern—a dripping Ben Gunn [*Treasure Island*] sporting a full salt and pepper beard. I said, "Kaoha!" He looked at me with a blank look. "Bonjour!" Nothing. In my Frañol [French-Spanish] I asked, "Do you fish?" He just dripped water into my dinghy and gave me an empty stare. "I'm Joe, what's your name?" Blank stare again and silence. I had just spent an hour doubled over the bow pulpit fixing a running light and I was thirsty. I asked him if he wanted something to drink. He nodded. Aha! He wasn't a deaf mute. Maybe mute, but not deaf. I asked his name again and he answered, "Mamaa'i Popiani." We got into a one-sided conversation about fishing as I handed him a few fishing hooks, which he accepted gracefully.

He slowly opened up as I showed him the boat. After the tour, I took him ashore in the dink in search of water, and found a water spigot next to a metal-roofed shed by the little concrete quay. The stand pipe was broken and the water flowed continuously, much to the delight of the papaya trees thriving downstream. I looked around for Mamaa'i but he had disappeared into the coconut groves along the side of the road without so much as a by-your-leave. I shrugged to myself and lugged the water jugs back to the dinghy. I had rowed about 10 yards off shore when Mamaa'i came running toward me with his arms full of coconuts. He was walk-running, taking long strides to keep the coconuts from falling but to no avail. The nuts kept falling and Mamaa'i kept stopping to pick them up, dropping a few more as he bent down. I turned around and rowed back to the quay where he silently handed me six husked coconuts, turned around and left. Three of the nuts were the young light-colored ones with the best water; some even seemed to be effervescent; the three others were ripe and good for making coconut milk. This simple kindness is typical of the Marquesan attitude toward visitors.

# HANAIAPA

About eight miles northeast of Hanamenu is another beautiful anchorage, Hanaiapa. Passing Point Matatepai, the "grand canyon" ends and you are again in the tropics where palms and greenery abound. The entrance to this anchorage is the only approach requiring a caution: *Don't hit the big rock* (Po'onika) at the entrance. It is a black obelisk with some white guano stains that, from a distance, look like graffiti. I don't recommend passing between Jouan Point and Po'onika. Although it looks like there's plenty of water, the rocks off Jouan Point are ominous. Soundings for the chart were taken by the H.M.S. *Beagle* in the 19th century, and I don't trust them.

Pay attention as you pass Matatepai Point just after the third cave in from the point, there is a beautiful waterfall free falling 250 feet, which I'm told runs all year. If you can take your eyes off the waterfall long enough not to plow into Po'onika, you will be rewarded with a nice little blowhole spraying regularly just past the rocks off Point Jouan. All those white dots on the cliff sides around you are goats.

## ⚓ ANCHORING TIPS

I prefer the anchor site on the eastern side by the little concrete dock where it should be a little less rolly, although there is not much difference anywhere in the bay. Anchor in 35 feet in good, old, black, sandy mud. Be sure to use both a bow and stern anchor when there is no breeze.

## 🏄 GOING ASHORE

You can tie your dinghy to the concrete dock or beach it on the sand bar formed by the stream outflow just to right of center of the beach. I recommend the dock (using a stern anchor) only because the walk around the bay is pleasant.

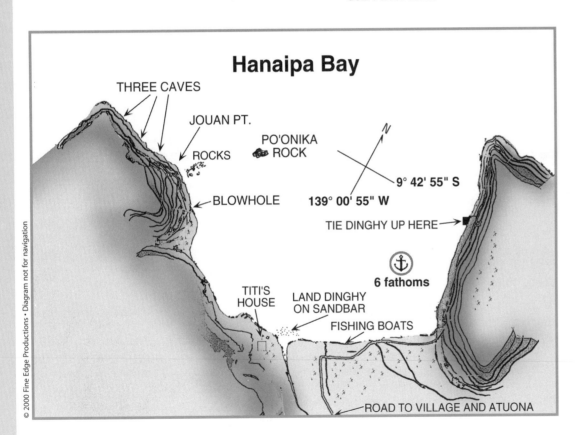

**Hanaipa Bay**

THREE CAVES
JOUAN PT.
PO'ONIKA ROCK
ROCKS
BLOWHOLE
9° 42' 55" S
139° 00' 55" W
TIE DINGHY UP HERE →
⚓ 6 fathoms
TITI'S HOUSE
LAND DINGHY ON SANDBAR
FISHING BOATS
ROAD TO VILLAGE AND ATUONA

© 2000 Fine Edge Productions • Diagram not for navigation

# Hanaiapa

*(Hah-nah-ee-ah-pah)*

The village of Hanaiapa lies up the road a few hundred yards inland. Monica and Mike Brown, crew of the cutter *Capella* enjoyed spending time with William, a local resident and well known "cruiser-o-phile" who has lived in the village for years. He has a guest book signed by hundreds of yachtsmen; be sure to visit him.

A request: Just south of the blowhole on the west side of the bay, there is a cave partially submerged at low tide. If anybody wants to get wet, check it out and give me a report.

Speaking of snorkeling, the clarity of the water in Hanaiapa is superb and night divers will find lobster in the rocks and coral below the cliffs in the bay. Be aware that there are seasons for lobstering. The Marquesans respect those seasons and expect you to do the same.

Po'onika Rock

Cruisers rowing ashore in paradise

## The Power of Tapu (Ancient Laws)

An influential and somewhat skeptical official of the Marquesan education department learned that a school construction crew in Hatiheu on Nuku Hiva had come across a stone tiki. The tiki was in the way of the remodeling and the official decided to commandeer the statue as a decoration for his own house on Hiva Oa.

Shortly after installing the female tiki at his home, he began experiencing psychological problems that became so severe he had to quit his job and enter a hospital in Tahiti. The man's wife knew the tiki was the cause and asked Ozanne Rohi to take the tiki back to Hatiheu in his fishing boat. Ozanne reluctantly agreed to help, but never intended to let that stone bitch get aboard his own boat. He attempted to sneak the tiki aboard the *Aranui* but the skipper caught wind of the plan and turned him back at the gangplank. Ozanne was successful in spiriting the stone image aboard the *Taporo* and back to Nuku Hiva, where he handed the tiki over to the mayor of Taiohae. The mayor restored her to the exact spot in Hatiheu from which she was taken. Within a month, the school official had recovered and was back at work.

The moral here is don't mess around with "live" tikis or the captain of the *Aranui*.

# Chapter 6
# FATU HIVA

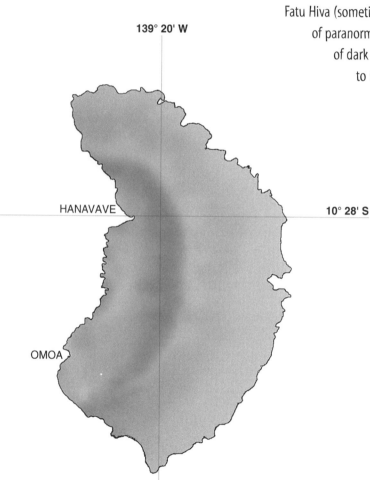

Fatu Hiva (sometimes pronounced Fatu Iva) is a mysterious place. I am not one to buy into the world of paranormal pablum, but every picture I have ever taken of the island has a disconcerting aura of dark eerieness. Thor Heyerdahl spent nearly a year here in the 1930s and though he tends to use hyperbole, he also mentioned the feeling of unease that the island causes. The people, of course, are as friendly as can be and the landscape is beautiful.

## Getting there

I suggest sailing to Fatu Hiva from Hiva Oa. You cannot check in at Fatu Hiva and getting there from any other island is normally a beat to weather. Leave Atuona, Taahuku Bay, at 7 a.m. or before. If you leave any later you may find that the wind has piped and clocked to the south, making the trip uncomfortable.

Plan on motoring east along the southeast coast of Hiva Oa. Putt along for as long as is comfortable or until you are sure you can lay the southwest point of Mohotani (Motane) Island. Keep clear of the cliffs on Mohotani or you'll find yourself in a wind shadow which alternately produces dead calms or williwaws that can knock your boat on its beam ends.

From Mohotani, hold a course of 120° to 130° for as long as the winds permit. Generally, in the southern summer (November-March) winds veer north in the afternoon. In the southern winter (June-September) winds back to the south in the afternoon.

As you approach Fatu Hiva, once you are parallel to its west coast and within a couple of miles of Hanavave, the winds become fluky, so you might as well crank up the iron staysail.

# HANAVAVE

*"Bay of Virgins"*

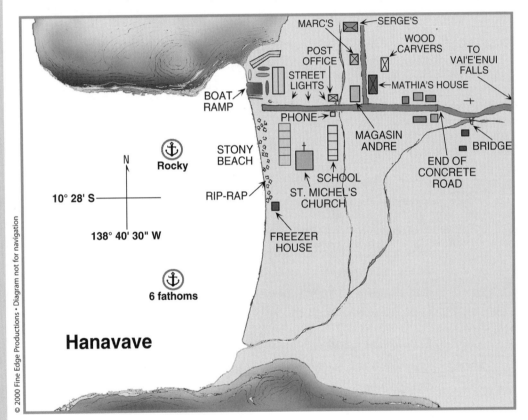

MARC'S
SERGE'S
POST OFFICE
WOOD CARVERS
TO VAI'E'ENUI FALLS
STREET LIGHTS
MATHIA'S HOUSE
BOAT RAMP
PHONE
MAGASIN ANDRE
BRIDGE
STONY BEACH
END OF CONCRETE ROAD
Rocky
SCHOOL
RIP-RAP
ST. MICHEL'S CHURCH
10° 28' S
138° 40' 30" W
6 fathoms
FREEZER HOUSE
N
**Hanavave**

© 2000 Fine Edge Productions · Diagram not for navigation

From a mile out, it is sometimes hard to discern the little Bay of Virgins. This cove, advertised in France as the most beautiful in the world, has sheer volcanic cliffs that meet the water fjord-style with lava turrets inspiring the name "Penis Bay." It didn't take the Catholic priests long to change its name to "Baie des Vierges."

## ⚓ ANCHORING TIPS

Anchoring is easy but the bottom near the north cliffs is fairly rocky and you may grind and drag a bit when gusts roll down the valley. Stick to the center of the bay away from the northern cliffs, where you will find good holding ground 35 feet down in sandy coral.

## 🚣 GOING ASHORE

After you have set the hook and absorbed the moonscape, you will want to get ashore. The only convenient dinghy landing is at the launching ramp in the northeast corner of the cove. It is important not to leave your dinghy *on* the ramp as fishermen regularly launch and beach their boats here. If you have a light rubber dinghy, don't mount its motor. Instead, row ashore and hoist the dinghy atop the concrete wall paralleling the ramp. Place it as far up the ramp as you can and it will be safe. If there is no room on the wall, schlepp it up and around to the south side of the ramp.

# Walking Tour: Hanavave

(Hah-nah vah-vay)

You can fill your water jugs at two spigots near the pirogues stored at the ramp; a garbage can is usually located on top of a piece of concrete rip-rap to keep the dogs out of it. Fuel is not sold in Hanavave but a friendly fisherman will usually sell you some gasoline or mixed outboard fuel.

There is only one paved road which runs straight east from the ramp area. The easiest way to give directions around greater metropolitan Hanavave is to use the streetlights. There are six of import to the cruising tourist.

As you walk up concrete "Main Street," St. Michel's Catholic Church is on the right. The mass starts here at 8:00 a.m. on Sunday. If you get to church half an hour early, you can listen to the ukelele and guitar group practicing. The wonderful Polynesian harmonies heard at the mass reinforce my

contention that all Marquesans can sing. Maybe it's in the genes and they all have perfect pitch. Or maybe the ones that cannot sing are just told to keep quiet.

Adjacent to the fourth street light from the ramp is the post office which is no more than a light-green wooden shack with a piece of plywood hinged to form the service window. Across the street stands the telephone booth where calls can be made worldwide.

There are about 80 children in the school behind the telephone booth. The kids represent roughly half the total population of Hanavave. When school is out, you may end up being a modern Pied Piper dragging a train of youngsters around chattering, "Bonbons" (candy). They aren't pests or persistent, but it is the only place in the Marquesas where the kids ask you for anything. What the kids enjoy most is a visit to your boat. Each day we invited a *few* kids out for cookies and soda. They were always well-behaved and their presence is one of the highlights of a trip to Hanavave.

Continuing up the street a couple of lights (six) you come to the corner of Main and Dirt. On one corner is **Magasin André**. Although this could not be called the best stocked supermarket in the Marquesas, I *have* seen a cold Hinano and a bottle of Best Foods mayonnaise.

Turning left up Dirt Road, the last house on the left is Serge Kohueinui's home. It has to be large to house Serge, his wife Kati, his parents, two sisters Gislaine and Sophie and his two kids, Lorena and Serge Jr. The Kohueinui family is prominent in the village and Serge is a good contact. He is a wood carver who will show you his hand-carved ukeleles, tikis, hair harpoons, etc. Sophie makes tapa cloth, as do several other women in the village. Serge will be happy to introduce you to all of them.

Fatu Hiva is the last island in French Polynesia where tapa cloth is still made. Tapa is made by peeling the bark off one of several species of trees. These relatively dry strips of bark are soaked and kept wet while being pounded thin with wooden mallets over a log. Walking through Hanavave on a peaceful afternoon with the sound of women pounding tapa and teenagers playing ukeleles is a unique experience.

Serge's brother Marc is also a carver and lives nearby. Sopi, another brother and a fisherman, lives behind Serge. He can supply you with fish at the going rate but you must buy the whole fish. He normally keeps his tuna in the fish freezer near the boat ramp until the *Aranui* arrives to take it to Papeete. The price for Yellow Fin is twice as much in Tahiti.

The paved road eventually turns into the path to Vai'e'enui Falls. On the way up you pass Mama Kahiha's house, a delightful woman who lives in the last house up the valley.

Her daughter is the local postmaster. Past Mama Kahiha's house the trail ends and the rest of the jungle route is marked only by small stones stacked atop huge lava boulders, some of which have been stacked there for decades. If he has time, Serge will guide you on the 1.5-hour trek up the valley to the 300-foot free-drop waterfall into an olympic-sized, kidney-shaped pool. When you reach the falls you will find the water is colder than hell but it is welcome after the humid march up the mountain.

Eric Van Hammersveld, skipper of *Ti'Ama* and a man of few words, once made a less than stunning but accurate observation about Hanavave. We were strolling down Main Street in Hanavave on a quiet, sunny afternoon when he suddenly stopped and blurted out, "There's no road kill here!" That was Eric's way of noting there are no cars in Hanavave. At the time of his remark, there was only one car on the island and that was in Omoa. Now there are about eight cars in Omoa. I suppose some people would consider that to be progress.

Vai'e'enui Falls

# Chapter 7

# TAHUATA

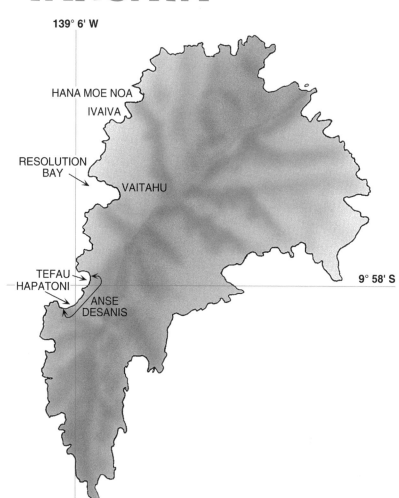

139° 6' W

HANA MOE NOA
IVAIVA

RESOLUTION
BAY

VAITAHU

TEFAU
HAPATONI

ANSE
DESANIS

9° 58' S

## *Tahu* = fire, *ata* = spirit

The land of poor Chief Iotete and his tribe was the first landfall of the Spaniards' *Mendaña*, and the site where Marquesans were first affected by the arrival of the *hao'e* (white man). Historic and beautiful, Tahuata has several wonderful overnight anchorages that you will remember long after you depart the archipelago.

# HANA TEFAU & HAPATONI BAY

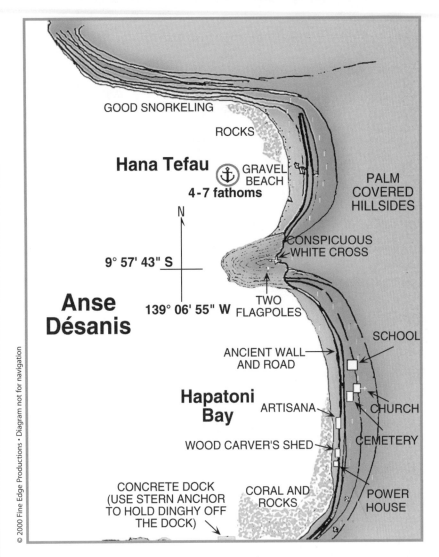

GOOD SNORKELING

ROCKS

**Hana Tefau** ⚓ GRAVEL BEACH
**4-7 fathoms**

PALM COVERED HILLSIDES

N

9° 57' 43" S

CONSPICUOUS WHITE CROSS

**Anse Désanis**

139° 06' 55" W

TWO FLAGPOLES

SCHOOL

ANCIENT WALL AND ROAD

**Hapatoni Bay**  ARTISANA

CHURCH

WOOD CARVER'S SHED

CEMETERY

CONCRETE DOCK (USE STERN ANCHOR TO HOLD DINGHY OFF THE DOCK)

CORAL AND ROCKS

POWER HOUSE

© 2000 Fine Edge Productions • Diagram not for navigation

Since sailing from Atuona, Taahuku Bay, down the Bordelais Channel is an easy and delightful trip, I won't describe it as a route to western Tahuata. However, if you are sailing from Fatu Hiva, set a starboard tack and head for Cape Tehopeotekeho on the southern tip of Tahuata.

When rounding Tehopeotekeho, Désanis Cove (Anse Désanis) is always closer than I expect. The chart scale is visually deceiving to me (and apparently only to me). So just use the ol' G.P.S. and you won't pass it up as I frequently do.

Hana Tefau and Hapatoni Bay are two bays in Désanis Cove. Between the two bays there is a rock promontory with a conspicuous white cross and two flagpoles on top.

## ⚓ ANCHORING TIPS

Drop the hook in Hana Tefau in 25 feet on a rock/sand bottom. The wind swirls here so stand well off the rocks. I once put out five-to-one scope in 40 feet of water and found myself perilously close to the rocks when a squall rolled in from seaward. It scared the hell out of me one dark and stormy night.

Though hard to find, there is one small, acceptable anchor site in Hapatoni Bay. It is close to the concrete dock and the reef in 40 feet (12 meters). I looked for it after a French cruiser had left the spot but only found 90 feet in coral. Keep looking, you may find it. Otherwise, do what the rest of us do, anchor over in Hana Tefau.

## 🚶 GOING ASHORE

Anchoring in Hana Tefau has one drawback. It's a 'fer piece' over to the concrete dock at Hapatoni. The beach, guarded by a coral reef, is rocky. If you are rowing, get a tow. However you get there, tie up to the quay and drop a stern anchor to keep your dink from banging against the rough concrete.

# Walking Tour: Tefau/ Hapatoni

*Fau* is the fiber from the bur'au plant used in ancient times for strapping outrigger canoes together. Today it is used to hang bananas by their stalks. *Hapatoni*, on the other hand, is Marquesan pasta.

No fuel can be purchased in Hapatoni or Tefau. Water can be found only by asking a friendly Marquesan but there is no place to dispose of garbage.

Walk east from the narrow quay turning left (north) on the ancient road that parallels the shore. This is undoubtedly one of the most beautiful and pleasant paths in the Marquesas if not the South Pacific—a palm-lined paradise. This thoroughfare, built in ancient times, is as wide as a modern street and lined with stone walls on either side.

A few hundred yards down the path, on the left, is an open shed adjacent to the powerhouse where most of the wood carvers congregate to work. Sebastian, Fermin, Timi, Amede and Emile who can usually be found at the shed by 7 a.m., will show you their current projects. Most of their works end up in Tahiti for the tourist trade.

Farther north, on the beach side of the road, is the beautiful new artisana where the works of the carvers are displayed and sold. Also sold there are dried bananas, preserved in the ancient fashion used by the Marquesans on their original voyages of discovery 1,700 years ago.

As you continue north, the little church is visible behind the small cemetery. The one-room schoolhouse is next on the right.

Upslope from the road in the coconut groves, several ancient *paepae* (stone platforms) are visible adjacent to a long stone wall. The road eventually turns into a path leading to the site of ancient tapu religious rites. The site has been taken over by a white cross, two flagpoles and a Catholic shrine.

Marquesan musicians and dancers

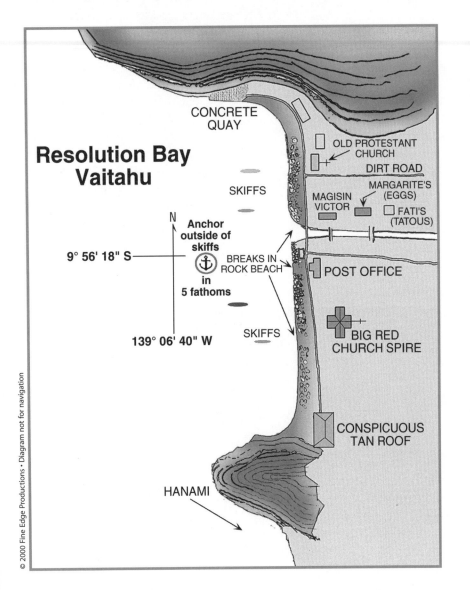

**Resolution Bay
Vaitahu**

CONCRETE QUAY

OLD PROTESTANT CHURCH

DIRT ROAD

SKIFFS

MARGARITE'S (EGGS)

MAGISIN VICTOR

FATI'S (TATOUS)

N

9° 56' 18" S

**Anchor outside of skiffs**

BREAKS IN ROCK BEACH

**in 5 fathoms**

POST OFFICE

139° 06' 40" W

SKIFFS

BIG RED CHURCH SPIRE

CONSPICUOUS TAN ROOF

HANAMI

© 2000 Fine Edge Productions • Diagram not for navigation

# RESOLUTION BAY

Motoring a few miles north of Hana Tefau, you will see a huge church with a red steeple just right of the center of the beach. You can't miss it. If this is what you see, odds are you are in Resolution Bay.

## ⚓ ANCHORING TIPS

There are no obstructions. One well-known cruising guide describes the holding ground as bad at Vaitahu. Wrong. Just stay outside the line of anchored skiffs and your hook will catch nicely in 30 feet of muddy sand.

## 🚣 GOING ASHORE

The best landing spot for your dinghy is on the beach at one of the three breaks in the rock rip-rap. If for some reason the surf looks like The Pipeline, throw a dinghy anchor in and Med-moor the dink at the quay. Otherwise, the best place to land is the right-hand break in the rocks. The northernmost (left) break in the rocks, the river outflow, is not good for landing. The next one to the right, closest to the post office, is okay except that pirogues park there and the flat above the beach can be crowded. There is plenty of room if you pull your dinghy ashore and haul it all the way up on the flat next to the plaque commemorating the first French arrival on Tahuata. A dinghy landing can be had at the concrete headwall on the north end of the waterfront, but I don't recommend it.

# Walking Tour: Vaitahu

*Vaitahu* means "fire water" or "water fire." Take your pick. *Vai* = Water, *Tahu* = fire.

Vaitahu is the main village on Tahuata. It is also the spot where Mendaña landed in 1595, killing 70 Marquesans.

Walk north on the strand road. The only building on the left side is the post office where you can find a telephone and fax service. The *mairie* (town hall) is in the same building as the post office and if you really need diesel, ask them and they may be able to help you find a small, emergency supply.

Across the street from the post office is the new school; inside its gate is a spigot where you can fill your jerry cans. The school is also the site of a small museum. I have never visited it as it seems to be closed a lot, so please send me a report if you have better luck.

The paved road up the valley parallels the river. There are two narrow foot bridges crossing the river from the road.

The first one leads directly to **Magasin Victor**. Although the shop is not very well stocked, you can purchase propane. You need a valve adaptor for your tank to be able to connect from the French system to the system you use on your boat.

The next bridge takes you to Marguerite's house as well as to Fati's house and the tatoo studio. Marguerite is a wonderful cook who sells eggs from her house. Fati is considered by many to be the finest tattoo artist in the Marquesas; he can also find fuel for you, and is a good contact as is Roger Animioi, his friend. (If you can find Roger Animioi in Vaitahu he may give you permission to visit the family land inland at Ivaiva.)

Up the road a bit is **Magasin Basinas** where you can also buy propane.

Generally speaking, it is better to stock your boat in Atuona or Taiohae than to depend on the shops in Vaitahu.

Vaitahu

## Prostitute's Bay

The anchorage at Vaitahu, Resolution Bay, was the site where Captain Cook landed and named the bay after his ship, *Resolution*. The anchorage, however, was given a lesser known name of *Baie de Putain*, or Prostitute's Bay, by the French.

Admiral Abel Dupetit-Thouars proclaimed the first French annexation of the Marquesas here. In 1842 Tahuata was the only island in the archipelago ruled by a single chief. This chief, Iotete (*Ee-oh-tay-tay*) was finally convinced it would be entertaining to swear allegiance to French King Louis-Philippe. The novelty wore off when Iotete realized that swearing allegiance meant the French could run rough shod over his people.

About this time, Iotete started feeling unwell and asked a priestess to diagnose his ailment. The priestess told him his problem was caused by the presence of the French. To make matters worse, the daughter of a prominent warrior was raped by one of the French sailors. The warrior retaliated by dispatching the Frenchman with a blow to the head with his *cassetête* (war club, literally a "head breaker") then fleeing to the hills after killing seven more soldiers who were hunting him down.

Meanwhile, Dupetit-Thouars had sailed off to bombard Tahiti into submission, leaving a young commander in charge of building a garrison at Vaitahu. This new commander demanded that Chief Iotete produce the warrior or he would fire to the village. Iotete responded by ordering the evacuation of Vaitahu, effectively stopping all work on the fort. The Admiral returned and let it be known that if Iotete did not reinhabit Vaitahu and surrender the warrior, he would chase him into exile never to see Tahuata again. Iotete's daughter, distraught and with no other way to save her father—offered her virtue in return for allowing her father to live in peace in the hills. The Admiral turned down the offer and demanded Iotete's return. The impasse was finally bridged when the warrior surrendered and Iotete repopulated Tahuata.

The name "Baie de Putain" was coined by the French sailors in commemoration of the offer of sexual favors Iotete's daughter made to save her father.

The person who told me this story also felt compelled to tell an apocryphal story about how—when Marquesans cannibalized their enemy—they only ate the thigh meat, whereas the Tahitians would roast the gonads of their foes and chow down. This preference was told to me to point out how civilized the ancient Marquesans were in comparison to the heathen Tahitians.

# ANCHORING AT A GLANCE

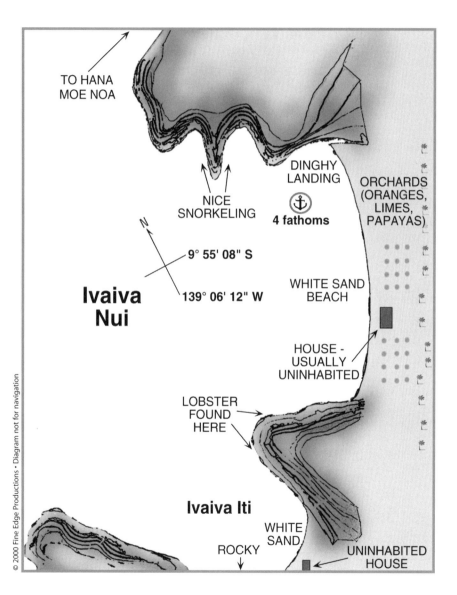

Diagram labels:

TO HANA MOE NOA

DINGHY LANDING

NICE SNORKELING

⚓ 4 fathoms

ORCHARDS (ORANGES, LIMES, PAPAYAS)

9° 55' 08" S

139° 06' 12" W

Ivaiva Nui

WHITE SAND BEACH

HOUSE - USUALLY UNINHABITED

LOBSTER FOUND HERE

Ivaiva Iti

WHITE SAND

ROCKY

UNINHABITED HOUSE

© 2000 Fine Edge Productions • Diagram not for navigation

# IVAIVA

(Ee-vah-ee-vah)

A few miles north of Vaitahu are the two idyllic bays of Ivaiva and Hana Moe Noa. The white, coral sand beaches resemble Caribbean wonderlands. The land behind Ivaiva is owned by the family of Roger Animioi and if you can contact him beforehand in Vaitahu, he may give you permission to go ashore where you can relax in peace and enjoy the solitude.

Ivaiva is first, but is not as protected as Moe Noa. There are no facilities at Ivaiva Nui and the land is posted as private but no one minds if you use the beach. If you want to walk inland, however, be sure to ask Roger Animioi.

## ⚓ ANCHORING TIPS

Anchor on the left side of Ivaiva Nui in 20 feet of water. The bottom is steeper than normal and the sand is thin atop a hard coral bottom in depths less than 20 or 25 feet.

## 🛶 GOING ASHORE

Land your dinghy on the far left side of the beach. Ivaiva Iti is not recommended for anchoring.

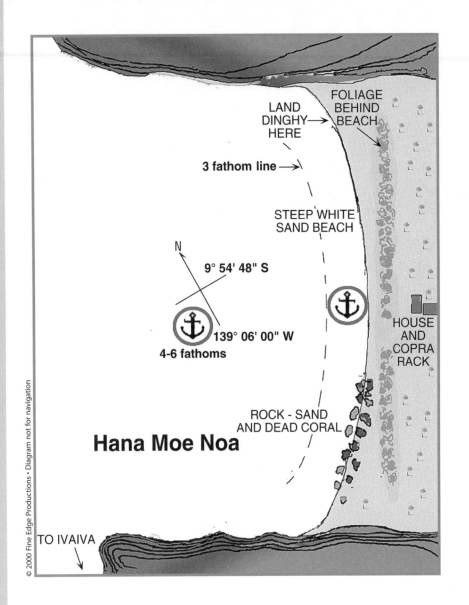

LAND DINGHY HERE

FOLIAGE BEHIND BEACH

3 fathom line →

STEEP WHITE SAND BEACH

N

9° 54' 48" S

139° 06' 00" W

4-6 fathoms

HOUSE AND COPRA RACK

ROCK - SAND AND DEAD CORAL

**Hana Moe Noa**

TO IVAIVA

© 2000 Fine Edge Productions • Diagram not for navigation

# HANA MOE NOA

A few miles north of Vaitahu are the two idyllic bays of Hana Moe Noa and Ivaiva.

Moe Noa is more protected than Ivaiva. There is no particular permission needed to go ashore at Moe Noa and there are no structures here. *Moe Noa* which means "long sleep" in Marquesan has no facilities.

## ⚓ ANCHORING TIPS

I prefer to anchor on the left (north) side of the bay in 20 or 25 feet.

## 🚣 GOING ASHORE

Land your dinghy on the north (left) end of the beach where it is calmer and the sand is not so steep.

**Note:** There are NoNos on the beach here so any daytime exploration should definitely be undertaken only with an ample supply of monoi oil or other effective anti-NoNo juice.

An evening *kaikai* on the beach at Moe Noa is a beautiful experience. As the sun goes down so do the NoNos and, in clear weather, you can see the spires of Ua Pou to the west. If there are no clouds on the horizon, the Green Flash supposedly can be experienced just as the sun drops out of sight. (Personally, I don't buy this Green Flash thing. I think people who have seen it were drinking too much beer as the sun receded.)

# Chapter 8

# UA HUKA

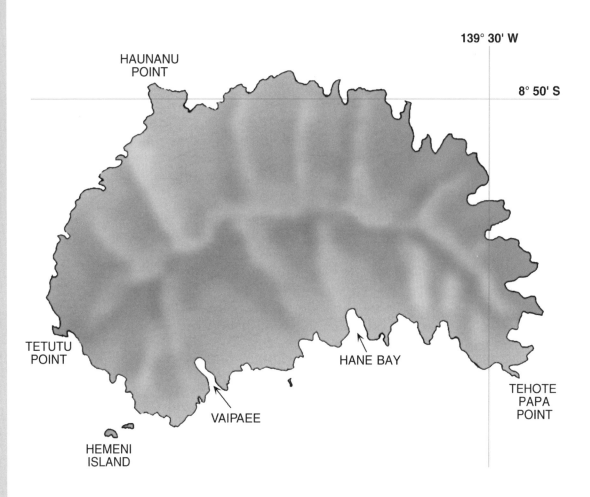

139° 30' W

8° 50' S

HAUNANU
POINT

TETUTU
POINT

HANE BAY

VAIPAEE

HEMENI
ISLAND

TEHOTE
PAPA
POINT

Neatness: that's the byword in Hane and the other parts of this industrious island; and in an island group noted for cleanliness, Ua Huka stands out as the shining example. The fertile citrus and coconut groves are another unique feature of this friendly Marquesan island.

# HANE BAY

[aka Titi'ea]
(*Tee-tee-eh-ah*)

When you take Motu Hane to starboard it doesn't feel like you have entered a well-enclosed anchorage. That's because you haven't. In unsettled weather, 35-40 knot winds howl between Motu Hane and the adjacent point, sometimes making Hane Bay uncomfortable.

But since you are here, you might as well anchor for the night; the closest alternative is to sail on to Vaipaee.

So, take pyramidal Motu Hane rock to starboard. (I don't think it's 508 feet tall, but what do I know?)

## ⚓ ANCHORING TIPS

A white sand bottom in 30 feet makes anchoring no problem. If there is no wind to hold your bow or stern toward the swell, whip out your stern anchor and point your bow about 120° to keep her comfy.

## 🚣 GOING ASHORE

The only reasonable place to land a dinghy is on the sandbar created by the river at the east end of the beach. Although some boaters have said the landing is difficult, I found *landing* was usually a piece of cake but returning back through the surf can be tricky. If the wind is piping, speed is of the essence. In this case, it may be better to have one person row or motor quickly through the surf and meet the other people at a chunk of concrete on the rocks 100 yards southeast of the sand bar. The concrete is shaped like a ramp and is past the breakers.

When you reach the shore, pull your dinghy up on the stony part of the beach; then get ready for the kids who will play on your dink if school is out. There is no sense getting your steam in an uproar; dinghies are fair game for Marquesan kids and your stream of unintelligible gringo isn't going to change countless generations of ardent dinghy players. Besides, they're not going to hurt your dinghy anyway.

**Note:** There is no water spigot near the dinghy landing so it might be better to get water at Vaipaee.

### Map labels

MAGASIN JEAN FURNIER
END OF CONCRETE RD
MAGASIN EDOUARD
SCHOOL
USUALLY DRY CREEK
STONE CARVER
STONE WALLED TERRACES
ARTISANA
ROAD TO VAIPAE'E
ROCK SEAWALL
DINGHY LANDING AT RIVER SAND BAR
CHUNK OF CONCRETE USED AS A RAMP
ROAD TO HOKATU
N
4-6 fathoms
8° 55' 36.3" S
139° 32' 05.5" W
**Hane Bay**
MOTU HANE

© 2000 Fine Edge Productions • Diagram not for navigation

# Walking Tour: Hane

The first things you notice on shore are stone terraces behind the seawall. Usually horses graze there and the scene is rather pastoral. Another thing you will notice about Hane is its neatness. The grass is trimmed and the streets are cleaner than most Marquesan towns which are already among the cleanest in the South Pacific. Neat rock walls line the concrete main road. There are only 160 inhabitants in Hane and 153 in the neighboring village of Hokatu.

Walking west from the sand bar, the first building you encounter is the *artisana*. Wood carving is the specialty of Hokatu, 2 km east. The products of their labor are displayed at the artisana. Delphine Rohotuehine, a school teacher in Hokatu, also works at the artisana; her husband, a sculptor, always has pieces on display. Delphine will be happy to escort you through the artisana or through Hokatu to watch the carvers at work.

As you continue up the concrete main street, you will come to a small bridge over a creek; it is usually dry. To the left is Joseph Tehau's outdoor stone carving "studio" where no-nonsense, anatomically correct tikis are created from large

pieces of native stone. Joseph's sculptures are purchased throughout Polynesia. If you can schlep one of these back to your boat, you'd better be sure you have a big boat!

Ua Huka sets a new and refreshing standard for signage—there are no signs for anything. So finding the first *magasin* is difficult, even when given explicit directions. I found myself standing in front of the first one asking directions to *it*.

On the left side of the main road where the concrete ends there is a dirt driveway. Take a left up the driveway, past the first house on the right. When you get to the second house, ask for directions (or figure you are already there so you can avoid looking stupid asking for directions to a location at which you have already arrived.) You have stumbled upon **Magasin Edouard** which carries a limited but adequate stock of grocery items. If you have a French adapter, you can purchase propane; small quantities of gasoline and diesel can also be obtained. Catherine and Edouard Teikihualanaka who own the store will allow you to buy merchandise from them even if you cannot pronounce their last name.

Back to the main road and across the next little bridge is the Catholic church to the left. **Magasin Jean Furnier,** another 1/4 mile up the road, carries the same goods as Magasin Edouard. No signs again, *bonne chance*.

# VAIPAEE BAY

*(Vai-pie-eh)*

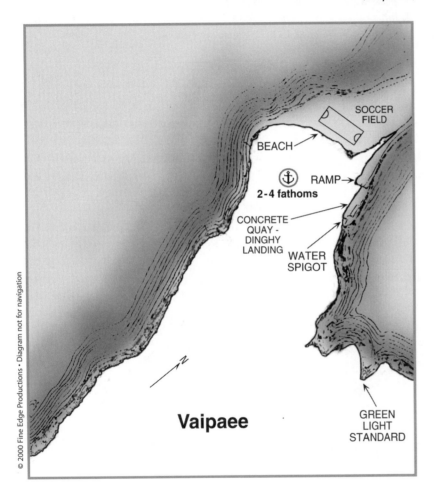

SOCCER FIELD

BEACH

⚓ RAMP→
2-4 fathoms

CONCRETE QUAY - DINGHY LANDING
WATER SPIGOT

Vaipaee

GREEN LIGHT STANDARD

© 2000 Fine Edge Productions • Diagram not for navigation

The southwest coast of Ua Huka is desert covered with scrub grass. Sheer cliffs buttress the sea with no discernable anchorages. But hold it! About three miles west of Hane Bay, someone planted a green standard on the side of a cliff to mark the eastern approach to Vaipaee. Upon closer inspection there is a light atop this standard. As you enter, taking the standard to starboard (remember it's "green right returning" in the Marquesas), the sides of the cliff close in until the opening is barely 100 yards inside. This fjord carves a mile deep into southwest Ua Huka.

## ⚓ ANCHORING TIPS

Near a concrete dock built on the eastern cliff side, the bay widens slightly. Anchorage can be taken here in 2 to 4 fathoms of muddy sand. A roll snakes its way into the anchorage and there is precious little swinging room, so even if you are the only boat in the bay, it is best to splash your stern anchor.

## 🚣 GOING ASHORE

There is a dinghy ramp north of the quay and a beach heads the bay. I prefer to land at the concrete quay, throwing out a stern anchor, but the ramp can be used as well.

**Note:** There are two water spigots on the quay but the pressure is very low and it takes some time to get 20-liter jerry cans filled. Also, the water though wholesome, suffers from a particulate problem. It is a bit muddy so if you have enough water aboard, wait to fill your tanks elsewhere. Send me a report if this situation improves.

# Walking Tour: Vaipaee

The ever-present soccer field is to the left as you stroll up the dirt road leading the quay. When there are no children kicking a ball around, you may see the ubiquitous white-"stockinged" horses grazing. Someone must have imported a different strain of horse here; I have not seen these stockings on horses of other Marquesan islands.

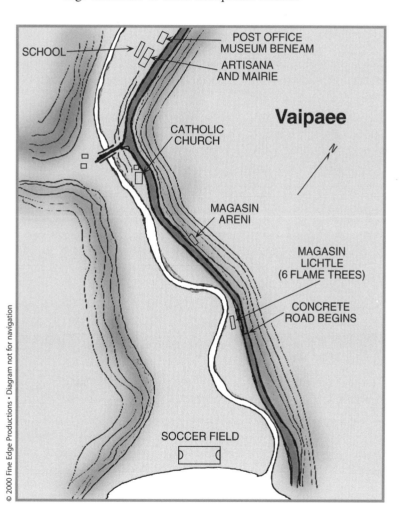

SCHOOL

POST OFFICE
MUSEUM BENEAM

ARTISANA
AND MAIRIE

Vaipaee

CATHOLIC CHURCH

MAGASIN ARENI

MAGASIN LICHTLE (6 FLAME TREES)

CONCRETE ROAD BEGINS

SOCCER FIELD

© 2000 Fine Edge Productions • Diagram not for navigation

Where the river nears the road, concrete paving begins and to the left are six Flamboyan trees which hide **Magasin Lichtle** (*Lisht-lay*). Marie Brown works in the store which is a long metal prefab building of obvious military origin. Propane is sold here but they do not have an adapter for the American system (that reverse-thread, knuckle-killer). Small amounts of diesel and gasoline are available. Credit cards are not accepted.

As you walk north you may notice an inordinate number of copra racks but few coconut palms. The plantations are inland and if you look far into the valley, a more verdant setting is visible. The inland areas also have beautiful banana plantations that are worth visiting. By the way, for you sailing ornithologists, Ua Huka has its very own birdy, the Marquesan Lorakeet called *Pihiti*, a little 18 cm., blue parrot-like bird which I never seen.

A few hundred yards north of Magasin Lichtle is **Magasin Areni**. And, lo and behold, it's got a sign! It sells the standard fare, including frozen chicken but no propane or other fuel. There is an aggravating aspect of Ua Huka I want to point out. Hinano is not sold in bottles there. Picture yourself, or me, schlepping an empty case of Grand Hinanos all over Vaipaee, wandering in vain from *magasin* to *magasin* asking for a refund on the bottles and the plastic case. Somebody must have it in for Hinano. Magasin Areni had three or four small cans but no bottles and no interest in taking 20 bottles off my hands. The deposit is 60 cents per bottle plus $6.00 for the case. That is $18, and I wanted my dough, but in Ua Huka I was wasting my time.

On up the road, the river again closes on the road and a fork made of the river and the road cradles the Catholic church, The Virgin of the Immaculate Conception.

Another 100 yards north is the *mairie*, well kept with groomed gardens. The island's government offices and the adjacent compound make the walk worthwhile. A plaque in the garden commemorates Etienne Marchand's landing on Ua Huka in 1791, when he named the island after his ship, *Le Solide*. Reliable sources report that he never really bothered to visit Ua Huka and that he lied about the visit in his log.

The *mairie* is made up of two buildings. The one on the left houses the mayor's office and an artisana. The artisana displays the carvings of the men of Hokatu and others. The last time I was there, an intricately sculpted ho'e (canoe paddle) was displayed and priced at $500 (50,000 CFP). It was magnificent and well worth the price. The other building is a two-story affair which houses the museum downstairs and the post office above. Access to the post office is at the street level. Beyond a doubt, Vaipaee has the best museum in the Marquesas. It is well-organized, with plenty of authentic pieces, not just replicas. Of particular interest are the three ancient wooden tikis on loan from the Teikihuavanaka family (remember them from Magasin Edouard in Hane?). Do not, under any circumstances, miss this beautiful little museum. And, as are the best things in life (except boats), it's free.

**Note:** *During one visit here, I was told that a guy living behind the church sells diesel but I could never find him.*

Sailing out of Vaipaee toward the west takes you past Joseph Lichtle's property at Haavei. I have never visited this open road but was told at the mairie that permission to land is readily available from Mr. Lichtle at Haavei. (Joseph is the father of the mayor of Ua Huka, Leon Lichtle.)

## The Arrival of the Aranui

If you can ever arrange to be anchored in Vaipaee when the *Aranui* arrives, grab a beer, sit back in the cockpit and watch the show. Based in Tahiti, the beautiful white *Aranui* and the less beautiful but equally industrious red *Taporo*, are the two copra steamers that ply French Polynesia. They carry cargo and passengers to the Marquesas returning with a hold filled with copra.

Trying to turn the *Aranui* around inside the narrow fjord is quite an event. They send the passengers on to Hane in cars while they turn the ship around and pick them up on the way to Hokatu.

Unloading a car from the ship is particularly exciting as they hoist the auto onto a ramp placed athwart two outboard-powered longboats tied together. Then, a budding Evel Knievel drives the car off the ramp at full speed, wheels a-chirpin'. At the moment when the main weight of the vehicle is transferred from the longboat-raft to the dock, the longboats raise up and throw the back of the car into the air where it loses some traction. Rear wheel drive cars are the most fun to watch. What a show!

# Chapter 9

## UA POU

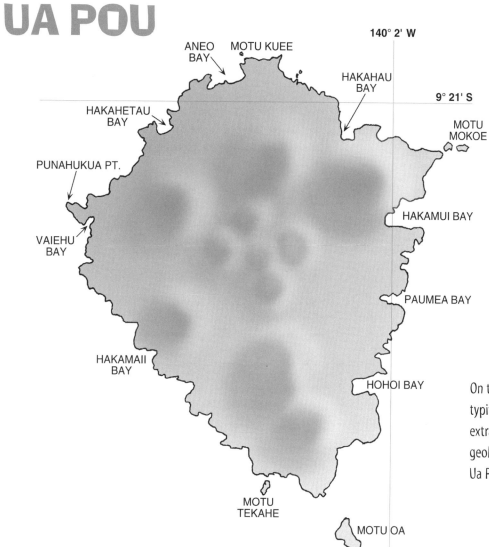

140° 2' W

ANEO
BAY

MOTU KUEE

HAKAHAU
BAY

9° 21' S

HAKAHETAU
BAY

MOTU
MOKOE

PUNAHUKUA PT.

HAKAMUI BAY

VAIEHU
BAY

PAUMEA BAY

HAKAMAII
BAY

HOHOI BAY

On the island of Ua Pou (*Poe* not *Pooh*) the people
typify the graciousness of Marquesan society. What is
extraordinary is the skyline. Arguably the most striking
geological formations on the planet, the spires of
Ua Pou are magnificent.

MOTU
TEKAHE

MOTU OA

# ANCHORING AT A GLANCE

## HAKAHAU BAY
*(hah-kah-how)*

As you take the breakwater to port, again remember in the Marquesas it's red left returning. A red light standard sporting a one-second flasher adorns the end of the stone breakwater.

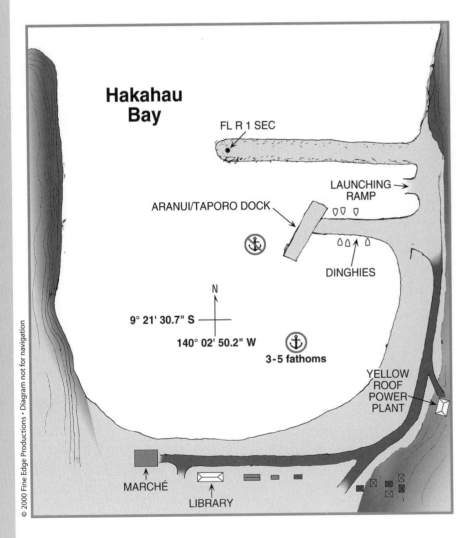

Hakahau Bay

FL R 1 SEC

LAUNCHING RAMP

ARANUI/TAPORO DOCK

DINGHIES

N

9° 21' 30.7" S

140° 02' 50.2" W

3-5 fathoms

YELLOW ROOF POWER PLANT

MARCHÉ

LIBRARY

© 2000 Fine Edge Productions • Diagram not for navigation

### ⚓ ANCHORING TIPS

If you can take your eyes off the most dramatic skyline in the Pacific long enough to anchor the boat, you should not have any problems dropping the hook in Hakahau Bay; there are no hidden obstructions here.

As in Vaipaee on Ua Huka, watching the *Taporo* or the *Aranui* squeeze into this tiny harbor is amusing. Unless you know the schedule of the ships, do not anchor north of the south end of the concrete quay. Even if both ships have just departed, you never know when a French naval vessel might pay a visit and force you to go through the anchoring maneuver at a less-than-convenient time.

As you approach the beach, keep an eye on your depth; it shallows quickly. The holding is excellent. The bent stock of my stern anchor is mute evidence of the quality of the holding ground. It needed the efforts of Fred at Magasin Kamake in Taiohae to make it right again.

There are usually several boats anchored deep in the eastern crook of the bay; these are long-term "tenants" belonging to teachers at Collège Terre des Hommes or government employees. Therefore, your mission is to tuck your boat as far to the east as possible without playing bumper cars with the other yachts. If you do not get well east of the breakwater opening, you are in for a rolly night even with the obligatory fore and aft anchoring.

### 🚣 GOING ASHORE

Hakahau has the nicest dinghy dock in the Marquesas. Actually, it is the fishing boat dock but there is plenty of room to tie up your dink. I usually don't bother with a stern anchor for my dinghy as there is little swell here and the prevailing wind tends to hold the dinghy away from the quay.

# Walking Tour: Hakahau

There are several water spigots on the quay. This is a good time to use that three-foot piece of hose you brought along with you to fill your water jerry cans. Once when we tied *Christina* to the quay to fill tanks and wash down, the surge was formidable, and it was eerie watching the hull flex every time it rolled against the big, black rubber commercial bumpers lining the quay. In settled weather pulling up to the dock works fine and saves you a lot of time not having to schlep the jerry cans. You need about 50 feet of hose, however—the nearest spigot is on the other side of the dock.

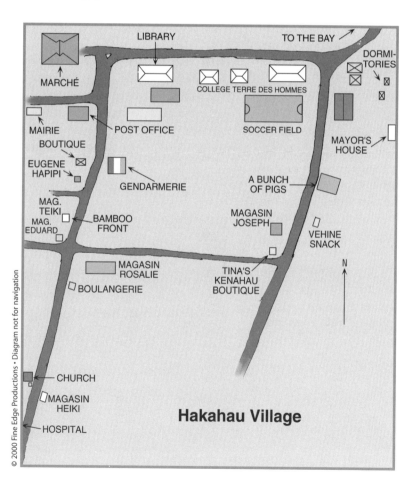

**Hakahau Village**

© 2000 Fine Edge Productions • Diagram not for navigation

You need to check in at the gendarmerie first, so walk to the base of the dock and start strolling toward town on the concrete road. You'll first pass the yellow-roofed power plant on your left. The rest of the buildings along the strand road belong to the Collège Terre des Hommes. The land and buildings—starting with the four bungalows (dormitories) on the hillside, to the library on the left at the end of the road—belong to the Collège.

At the library, the last building on the left, turn left. In about a quarter of a mile, you will find the gendarmerie on the left side of the concrete road.

In the vicinity of the gendarmerie (across the road) is the post office. One handy way to send news home is with an aerogram—a preprinted, folding letter. One page costs the same as a stamp but the pretty picture on the front is nice and the postage is included in the price. Just ask the person at the post office.

In front of the post office is the *marché*. Every so often, artisans display and sell their work at the marché. On Saturday nights they hold a dance and the band plays a combination of American and Marquesan music. When I say combination, I mean American rock and roll set to Marquesan words and beat. After a Hinano I might even describe it as exhilarating.

Fifty yards from the post office, down the side street, is the *mairie* where the bank can be found.

Across the road from the Gendarmerie is a boutique with goodies for the girls. Continuing south up the road you will come to a dirt road on the right. On the north corner lies the home of Eugene Hapipi. Eugene and his family are artisans and Eugene (pronounced approximately: *u-jen*) carves bone and wood tikis and talismans. The other members of the

Spires over Hakahau

clan twist coconut fiber into cordage for necklaces to be used to hold Eugene's amulets. He knows the other artisans in town and will be happy to show you where they work.

Back on the main road, on the right, is an unmarked bamboo building called **Magasin Teiki**, where propane and diesel can be found. One problem with buying propane here is they won't fill your tanks for you—you must do it yourself. Furthermore, you must buy a 12-kilo bottle and plunk down the deposit. Then, of course, you must have your own adapter. Some people hang the full bottle from a tree and let the gas drip into the empty one—a time-consuming operation as there is no pump like the one at your local gas station in the U.S.

It's about time to head to Rosalie's for a Hinano. Continue on up the road until you come to a cross street. Turn left and, *voilà*, on the right is **Magasin Rosalie**, a market and a restaurant where diesel and propane can also be purchased.

The boulangerie is around the corner, north of Rosalie's, on the same street as the Gendarmerie. By 9 or 10 a.m., the boulangerie is out of bread but you might find some in Magasin Teiki or Magasin Joseph until about noon.

Continuing up the road, the Catholic church is on the right followed by **Magasin Heiki** on the left. The only time I went to Magasin Heiki it was closed, but I've been told it is a well-stocked shop. The hospital is on the right a few hundred yards farther up the road.

Back down the road, turn right and walk down the road past Rosalie's. On the next corner is **Tina's Kanahau Boutique**. Tina Klima's prices are good; pareau here was almost half the price of that in Taiohae. You can buy cold drinks and souvenirs at Tina's and if your purchases are unwieldy, she will give you a handmade palm frond basket to carry your loot. The Kenahau Boutique is the only shop on Ua Pou that accepts credit cards; it is also a travel agency.

Next to Tina's is **Magasin Joseph** which even has a sign! This is the best-supplied store in Hakahau. A half liter of Hinano will get you through your browsing.

Head back to your boat walking north toward the strand road, passing a piggery on the right next to a thriving banana patch. The large building you see next on your left is the wood shop for the Collège Terre des Hommes. Here, kids up to the age of 15 are schooled before they are shipped off to Tahiti for any further education.

Beach at Hakahau

## *The* Aranui *and Lunch Chez Rosalie*

There is a true and well-kept secret about Rosalie's. If you time it to arrive at Hakahau to coincide with the *Aranui's* first arrival of the voyage, you might find yourself in cruiser's paradise. Here's the deal: When the *Aranui* departs Takaroa (Tuamotu) for the Marquesas, once a month or so, it first stops in Hakahetau on the west coast of Ua Pou, for a few hours to pick up copra before landing at Hakahau. The *Aranui* pays Rosalie to put on a spread for the first-class passengers. And what a spread it is! The buffet consists of lobster tails, *poisson cru* (excellent, nearly as good as my "World Famous Poisson Cru Recipe" q.v.), *chèvre au lait coco*, taro, tarua, fresh fruit—the works. Here's the best part. If you are a cruiser, Rosalie charges a ridiculously low price. Find out for yourself just how great the price is. The trick is to know when the *Aranui* is arriving for the first time on the current voyage. Also, arrive at Rosalie's early as she will have only a few tables left after the 60 or more passengers fill the place.

Currently, the *Aranui's* itinerary in the Marquesas is:

Ua Pou: Hakahetau, Hakahau
Nuku Hiva: Taipivai, Taiohae
Hiva Oa: Atuona;
Fatu Hiva: Hana Vave
Tahuata: Vaitahu

Then back to:

Hiva Oa: Puamau

For the first time to:

Ua Huka: Vaipaee, Baie d'Hane, Hokatu

Then back to:

Nuku Hiva: Anaho, Hatiheu, Taiohae
Ua Pou: Hakahau.

The *Aranui* itinerary completes in a week, so they don't mess around.

The Aranui

## HAKAHETAU BAY

*hock-ah-hay-tao*

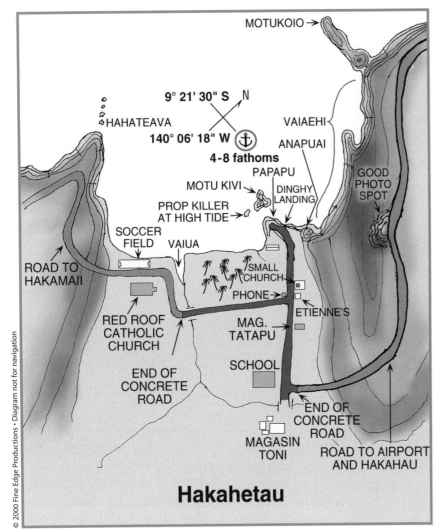

9° 21' 30" S    N

HAHATEAVA

140° 06' 18" W

4-8 fathoms

MOTUKOIO →

VAIAEHI

ANAPUAI

PAPAPU

MOTU KIVI

DINGHY LANDING

GOOD PHOTO SPOT

PROP KILLER AT HIGH TIDE →

SOCCER FIELD    VAIUA

ROAD TO HAKAMAII

SMALL CHURCH

PHONE →

ETIENNE'S

RED ROOF CATHOLIC CHURCH

MAG. TATAPU

SCHOOL

END OF CONCRETE ROAD

END OF CONCRETE ROAD

MAGASIN TONI

ROAD TO AIRPORT AND HAKAHAU

### Hakahetau

© 2000 Fine Edge Productions • Diagram not for navigation

Getting to Hakahetau Bay takes an hour or so of motor-sailing around the north end of the island and past the airport before you can duck into the cove.

The bay is cliff-lined. Directly in front of the concrete quay lies the monolithic Motu Kivi. It is small, but only in comparison to Anapuai, the mother of all naturally carved rocks. Motu Kivi is located directly behind the "dock"—a concrete pad poured over an outcropping of rocks named Papapu—that reaches toward Motu Kivi from the gravel beach.

### ⚓ ANCHORING TIPS

The first time I anchored here I dropped my hook too far toward the middle of the bay. I recommend anchoring more toward the northwest side where it is less rolly. Get as close to the northwest cliffs as is comfortable and anchor fore and aft facing about 350° to 340° magnetic.

The clarity of the water in the bay is good but the roll can be aggravating. Before the breakwater was built in Hakahau, about 60 to 70 yachts per year stopped in Hakahetau. Now less than half that number call here and this lack of traffic adds to the beauty of the bay.

### 🛶 GOING ASHORE

Getting ashore can be tricky. If you have a lightweight inflatable, take the engine off and row ashore taking Motu Kivi to starboard. Get off on the quay at the little ramp and haul your dinghy up onto the concrete. If that is not practical, bring a long painter (50 feet or so) and tie the bow to the light standard on the dock, dropping a stern anchor to hold your dinghy away from the rocks. There are no cleats on the concrete; when the *Aranui* comes in, it ties up to big bollards cast into the rocks. There is a possible landing on the southwest side of the quay on a small bit of beach where I have watched fishermen land, but there are rocks everywhere and there is a submerged prop killer west of Motu Kivi. I do not recommend landing here until you have more local knowledge about the conditions.

# Walking tour: Hakahetau

The backdrop to Hakahetau Bay is magnificent. Seven vertical basaltic spires—powerful giants—reign over the landscape. Oave, the tallest at over 3,900 feet, is the most "powerful" spire in the Marquesas. According to legend it was responsible for knocking down Matafenua, the peninsula on the eastern end of Hiva Oa which once stood upright and was something of a bully. Matafenua went stomping around knocking down all the spires on Nuku Hiva and Ua Pou. Oave would have none of this so when he grew up he marched right over to Hiva Oa and, after taking his wrath out on the smaller spires, knocked down Matafenua, chopped off his head and stuck it in his loin cloth where it resides today at his side, 600 feet below him. Of course, since we are now in the northern group, his name was changed to Matahenua. This is a true story, ask anybody.

Ambling up the road extending inland from the dock, you are on the only pavement in the village. I was first struck by the inordinate number of breadfruit trees in Hakahetau—many more than in most other Marquesan valleys. To increase copra (dried coconut meat from which coconut oil is extracated) production, the French encouraged the Marquesans to cut down breadfruit (me'i) to plant coconuts. There were two reasons for the decrease in breadfruit production. One, the dramatic decrease in population since French annexation of the islands caused a corresponding decrease in the demand for breadfruit. The influenza epidemic of 1863 alone wiped out half the population of the northern group not counting thousands more killed by venereal disease and tuberculosis. So, they did not need as much breadfruit. Secondly, the French decided it would be better for the Marquesans to buy beef and fish in a tin with the money earned from copra. And, since the average Marquesan would be working all day digging copra out of coconut shells, he wouldn't have time to dig *ma* pits for his popoi.

A short walk up the concrete finds you in front of the tiny Evangelical Church, founded in the late 19th century by the London Missionary Society.

Next door to the church is the **home/pension of Etienne and Ivonne Hokaupoko** *(hoke-ow-po-ko)*. My evenings with Etienne and Ivonne's are treasured memories. I first met Ivonne while I was browsing through Tina Klima's Kenahau Boutique in Hakahau one day. Ivonne is a Marquesan beauty who defies her age and the fact she has borne six children. She was accompanying two young Italian men to Tina's to buy airline tickets to Hiva Oa. The Italians who had "jumped ship" from the *Aranui* in Hakahetau, stayed at the Hokaupoko's pension for several days making friends; and they enjoyed it so much they missed the sailing from Hakahau and had to fly to Atuona to catch up with the little steamer. During our conversations, Ivonne had invited the crew of *Christina* to dinner at her home if we ever got to Hakahetau. Never being one to turn down an invitation for a kaikai, we arrived in Hakahetau the very next day.

Etienne—whose Marquesan name is Pua—is a wellspring of information on the history and legends of the Marquesas. As the president of the Marquesan Language Society, he has begun preparation of the only Marquesan/English dictionary, excerpts of which can be found in the glossary. When Etienne was a boy, he lived on Nuku Hiva and learned English from Bob McKittrick, Maurice McKittrick's father. You will read more about the inimitable Maurice in the Taiohae section.

The front yard of the Hokaupoko home has a large picnic table under an immense and prolific mango tree. Several years earlier, a lady cruiser, having completed a delicious dinner at the picnic table, was asked what she wanted for dessert. She thought for a moment and said, "A mango. That would be perfect." Then, as if on cue, a one-pound, ripe mango fell from the tree, landing with a thud on the table in front of her. Then and there a heavy duty *tapu* was placed on Etienne's tree.

A meal at Ivonne and Etienne's is always traditional—poisson cru, popoi, taro and tarua among other dishes—and everything is eaten with the hands. During the meal, Etienne, a former mayor of Hakahetau, will regale you with the history and legends of the islands while Ivonne keeps a steady stream of food flowing to the table. After dinner, the Hokaupokos will ask you to sign a huge guest book autographed by decades of world cruisers, famous as well as obscure.

Across the street from Hokaupoko's is a phone booth where you can place calls. Two houses up the street on the same side is **Magasin Tatapu**, unmarked, of course, except for one of those ubiquitous P&K Gum signs next to a sliding glass door into the shop. No beer here, but a small amount of general merchandise is available.

Continuing on, the school is the next conspicuous building and about 150 yards up the road. If you are lucky enough to arrive on a fête day, you will be treated to *tamure* (tah-mooray) dancing by the children. They are every bit as good as their elders. Apparently, like singing, tamure dancing is in the blood.

Past the school there is a bridge leading to **Magasin Toni**, the largest store in the village and well stocked.

Children assemble to dance at a school celebration

The concrete road ends here but if you recross the bridge and turn up the dirt road to Hakahau, a five-minute walk will reward you with an excellent spot for a photo of your boat in Hakahetau Bay. A rock outcropping where copra is sometimes spread out to dry makes a great platform for a snapshot.

Walk back to the phone booth and the intersecting road. Across the bridge spanning Vai Ua (two waters) and right, down the dirt road, puts you in front of the Catholic church. The fence in front of the church is covered with the most vivid lavender double bougainvilleas I have ever seen.

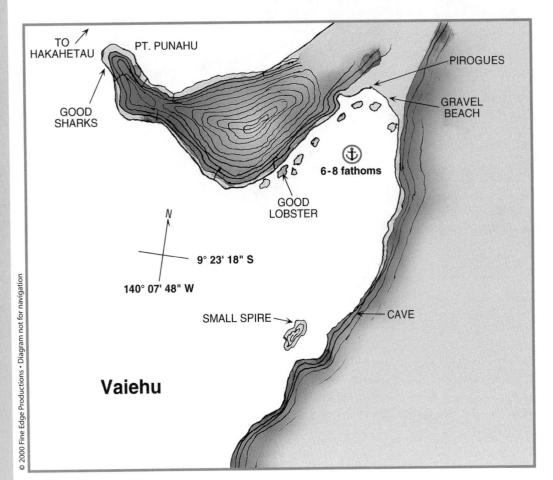

## VAIEHU BAY (VAIEO)

TO
HAKAHETAU

PT. PUNAHU

GOOD
SHARKS

PIROGUES

GRAVEL
BEACH

6-8 fathoms

GOOD
LOBSTER

N

9° 23' 18" S

140° 07' 48" W

SMALL SPIRE

CAVE

Vaiehu

© 2000 Fine Edge Productions · Diagram not for navigation

From Hakahetau to Vaiehu, Hahateava—the name of the pass between Hakahetau's southwest point, Tehena, and the rocks—is navigable only by fishing pirogues. Stay a safe distance from the rocks as you round the point and point the bow toward Point Punahu to the southwest.

Just before Punahu, the charming village of Haakuti is visible onshore. The dirt road from Vaiehu to Haakuti is conspicuous as it winds up the valley. As you round Punahu, you may see the dorsal fins of sharks feeding off the point. Stay clear of the northern cliff as you motor into the bay. The rocks along the cliffs are great for lobstering but bad for boat bottoms.

### ⚓ ANCHORING TIPS

Anchor as deep into the bay as you feel safe. I get itchy around rocks, so in Vaiehu I drop the hook in 50 feet. If by some quirk of El Niño the wind clocks to the west, get the hell out and have a nice downwind sail to Puamau (Hiva Oa). Normally, however, the wind whistles out of the pass dividing Point Punahu from the main body of Ua Pou. Let out plenty of scope so you can sleep peacefully before sailing up to Taiohae on Nuku Hiva.

# Chapter 10
# NUKU HIVA

Your first view and last recollection of Nuku Hiva will be of a seemingly surreal verdancy. Towering cliffs with fertile green folds are the hallmark of the Marquesas and this is especially true on Nuku Hiva. The cliffs lead down to a fan of alluvial deposits overgrown with acres of 60- to 100-foot tall coconut palms. The island seems to take on a new coat of deep green after every rainfall.

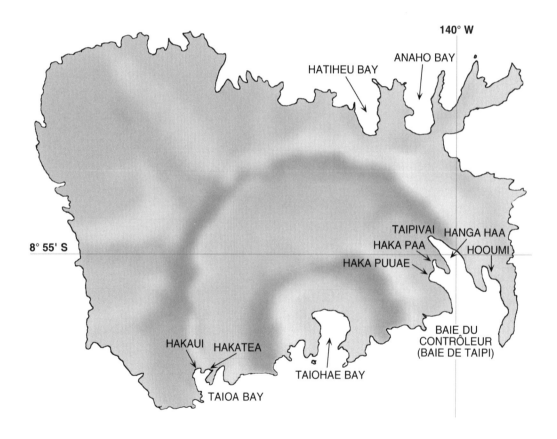

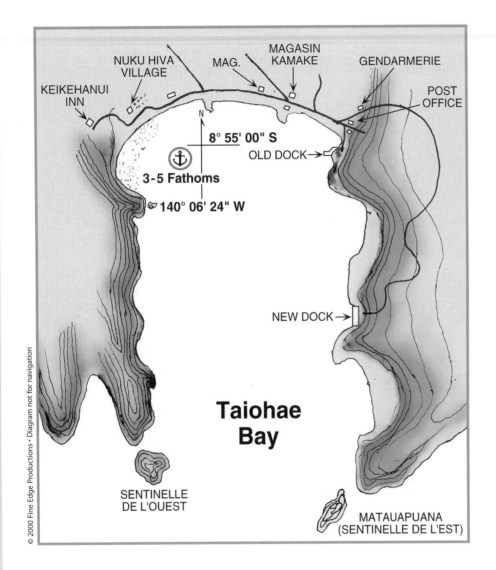

KEIKEHANUI
INN

NUKU HIVA
VILLAGE

MAG.

MAGASIN
KAMAKE

GENDARMERIE

POST
OFFICE

N

8° 55' 00" S

OLD DOCK →

⚓

3-5 Fathoms

⚓ 140° 06' 24" W

NEW DOCK →

Taiohae
Bay

SENTINELLE
DE L'OUEST

MATAUAPUANA
(SENTINELLE DE L'EST)

© 2000 Fine Edge Productions • Diagram not for navigation

## TAIOHAE BAY

Taiohae Bay, formed by the flooding of a volcanic crater, is straddled on both sides of its entrance by two small uninhabited islands, the Sentinelles. East Sentinel (Sentinelle de l'Est), also called Matauapuana, is to the right when entering. West Sentinel (Sentinelle de l'Ouest) is on the left. (Apparently Sentinelle de l'Ouest wasn't big enough to rate a local name.)

I have no qualms about entering Taiohae Bay at night if there is enough moonlight to discern The Sentinelles. The bay, deep to within 100 yards of the beach, has no invisible hazards. If you are unfamiliar with the bay, the only inconvenience to anchoring at night would be that—out of fear of running up on the beach—you end up anchoring in deeper water than you would during a daytime arrival. The charts show a range light emanating from the head of the bay but it has been intermittent at best, so don't rely on it.

Approaching Nuku Hiva

## ⚓ ANCHORING TIPS

Regardless of what some cruising guides may say, the yacht anchorage is in the **west** side of the bay in front of the school, cemetery and Nuku Hiva Village Hotel, and *not* on the eastern side. The eastern part of the bay is closer to the village shops and the gendarmerie, but the *Aranui* and *Taporo* maneuver in this area. Also, the large-vessel buoy in that area is regularly used by the navy. You will see the masts of the yachts anchored in the western part of the bay; so just anchor in an open space between them in 30 feet of sandy mud.

In the season of southerly winds, rollers sneak past The Sentinelles and make the anchorage uncomfortable. So, again, fore and aft anchoring is advised. Point your bow toward the entrance to the bay.

## 🛶 GOING ASHORE

As you look toward the shore you will notice some small fishing skiffs tied to buoys closer to the western beach. The best dinghy landing area is behind the skiffs. Take your dinghy up to, but no further west than, the last skiff-buoy then head directly into the beach. If you venture any farther west, you could find yourself bumping along the top of a coral reef. The reef is fully exposed during low tide, but many an outboard prop has been ruined here.

Pull your dinghy well up onto the beach and tie it to a tree limb. (Though I have never personally had a problem, you might consider tying up your dinghy with an old piece of wire rigging or a chain—many a yacht-braid painter has been "borrowed" to tie up a horse. However, your jerry can and dinghy motor will never be touched. Flip-flops can also get "lost" if left in a dinghy.) During a full or new moon, the waves reach the base of the trees, so be sure your dinghy is well tied. By the way, the only place I ever pitchpoled a dinghy was in Taiohae while beaching it at this location. It was during a high tide with an unusually heavy southerly swell. Be careful!

Taiohae Bay

There is another dinghy landing at the old quay on the other end of the bay. Although it's a long row from the anchor site, if you use an outboard on your dinghy, you could tie up here and be closer to town. There are showers and garbage receptacles on the old quay.

# Walking Tour: Taiohae

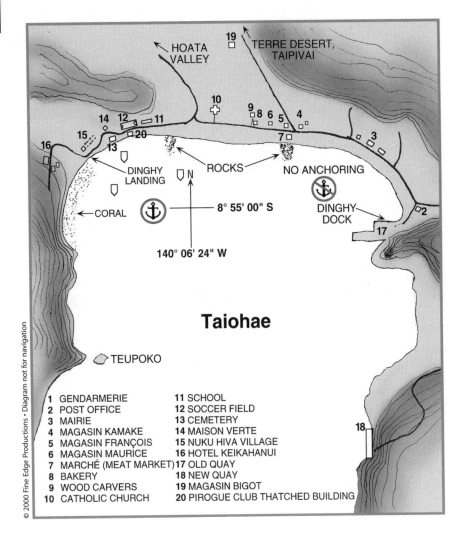

HOATA VALLEY

TERRE DESERT, TAIPIVAI

19

10

14 12 11

9 8 6 5 4

15

20

16 13

7

3

DINGHY LANDING

ROCKS

NO ANCHORING

N

2

8° 55' 00" S

DINGHY DOCK

CORAL

17

140° 06' 24" W

**Taiohae**

TEUPOKO

18

© 2000 Fine Edge Productions • Diagram not for navigation

| | |
|---|---|
| **1** GENDARMERIE | **11** SCHOOL |
| **2** POST OFFICE | **12** SOCCER FIELD |
| **3** MAIRIE | **13** CEMETERY |
| **4** MAGASIN KAMAKE | **14** MAISON VERTE |
| **5** MAGASIN FRANÇOIS | **15** NUKU HIVA VILLAGE |
| **6** MAGASIN MAURICE | **16** HOTEL KEIKAHANUI |
| **7** MARCHÉ (MEAT MARKET) | **17** OLD QUAY |
| **8** BAKERY | **18** NEW QUAY |
| **9** WOOD CARVERS | **19** MAGASIN BIGOT |
| **10** CATHOLIC CHURCH | **20** PIROGUE CLUB THATCHED BUILDING |

Taiohae is correctly pronounced *Ty-o-ha-eh* but most cruisers just say *Ty-o-hay*. Either way, Taiohae is the "capital" of the Marquesas and the most populated village in the archipelago.

Start your tour on the west side of the bay. The road along the beach leads from the Hotel Keikahanui property on the west to beyond the gendarmerie on the east. The **Hotel Keikahanui** is up the hill to your left as you face north toward the island. Frank and Rose Corser started building the original Keikahanui Inn almost 20 years ago catering to yachtsmen. They cruised extensively before "swallowing the anchor" to start the inn. They named the inn after a fierce tattooed Marquesan warrior who lived in Pua on the north shore and in Hakatea. Frank Corser passed away in 1992 and after that Rose carried on the tradition of welcoming yachties who used the inn as a mail drop during trans-Pacific voyages. When she and her partners sold the inn to Air Tahiti, the old buildings were razed. A new resort hotel, consisting of 20 bungalows, a gourmet restaurant, bar, and swimming pool, is now in operation. Amenities include air conditioning, television (with movies in French and English), and telephone.

Keikahanui Inn
B.P. 21 Taiohae
Nuku Hiva, Iles Marquises
Polynésie Française
Phone: (689) 920-710
Fax: (689) 920-711

Rose is an interesting character. In the days she owned the Keikahanui Inn, she went ballistic if you had sand on your shoes when you entered the restaurant. She still lives on the property downhill from the hotel where there is a boutique and museum. She has fax and telephone service and still serves as a good mail drop. You don't have to inform Rose of your arrival. Just give your friends the following address and your mail will be waiting when you get there.

Your Name
Your Yacht
c/o Rose Corser
B.P. 21 Taiohae
Nuku Hiva, Iles Marquises
Polynésie Française

Phone: (689) 920-382
Fax: (689) 920-074
E mail: rose.corser@mail.pf

The post office will send back any unclaimed general delivery mail after two weeks. Rose, on the other hand, knows that even the best planned itineraries can be thrown into chaos by the sea and winds not to mention the worst of all, the ITCZ spirits.

At the bottom of Rose's driveway you can buy cold beer at Bruno and Gloria Gendron's **Nuku Hiva Village Hotel**— the source closest to the anchorage. The Gendron (roughly pronounced *jon-drone*) family is prominent in both the Marquesas and the Society Islands.

Nuku Hiva Village is a collection of Polynesian-style thatched bungalows adjacent to a large thatched restaurant/ bar. Gloria takes care of the restaurant service and décor and Bruno handles the bungalows, grounds and, above all, the cooking. A great, gentle bear of a man, Bruno is a master in the kitchen and a full menu is available. The restaurant opens at 6 a.m. and closes at 10 p.m. except when a crowd is there—such as when Club Med flies a group in from Bora Bora for a three-day visit. Bruno puts on a big *kaikai* with a goat, pig and seafood barbecue complete with tamure dancers. The famous Marquesan Pig Dance is performed with

enthusiasm by a local dance group. Ask Gloria when the next group is due in and, if your cruising kitty can withstand the $30 to $40 bucks per person, reserve a table and enjoy the evening. Otherwise, you can enjoy the dancing by sitting on the lawn next to the restaurant when it's not raining or muddy. If you miss the big show, every Saturday night Bruno has a Marquesan band playing traditional music.

Sitting on the veranda at Bruno's with Gloria serving ice-cold Hinanos, surrounded by palm-frond roofs and tropical ambience, is the perfect way to celebrate the first evening on the island of Melville's "Typee."

Nuku Hiva Village
Phone: (689) 920-194
Fax: (689 920-597
Credit Cards are welcome

For a reasonable fee, Bruno will send and receive faxes for you and supply telephone service.

Up the dirt road toward town on the left before you reach the cemetery is the home of my Marquesan friends, Justin and Julienne. Justin works as the maintenance supervisor for the school on the beach and is a talented wood carver. His house, with a large blue roof, is almost invisible behind a beautiful garden and orchard.

A few yards more toward town, you will pass the cemetery on the right. Adjacent to the cemetery is a memorial to Herman Melville and Richard Tobias Greene, the two dirty, rotten ship-jumpers who fled the *Acushnet* to hide out in Taipivai for a couple of months. Melville's first book, *Typee,* is a loose narrative of his time there.

Heading east from the cemetery, the concrete pavement begins and a new pirogue club building has been built on the

View of valley outside Taiohae

beach across from the soccer field. The "Collège" (we would call it a junior high or middle school) is next to the soccer field. About a half-mile down the road is the corner where the road up Hoata Valley meets the strand. Just across the Hoata river bridge is **Snack Céline**, a nice little snack shop with a pool table.

Next you come to the head of the driveway leading to the Catholic church. It is believed the stone cross at the driveway marks the exact spot where the ancient Marquesans held human sacrifices. If you look closely, you will notice there is a cement joint between the top of the stone cross and the base. This is because the top of the monument originally depicted a rather explicit portion of the male anatomy. When the good fathers decided a phallic symbol was perhaps an inappropriate marquee for a cathedral, they had the most graphic portion of the monument replaced with a cross. Inside the church, the huge, carved wooden crucifix, altar and accoutrements are impressive examples of Marquesan wood sculpture. Everyone is welcome to enjoy the incredible music and traditions of the Marquesan Catholic Church during its Sunday services.

On the church property, there is an old building which houses the local FM station, Radio Meitai (*may-tai*). It broadcasts on 101.3 Mhz and plays a mix of American and Polynesian music. You know you are getting close to the islands when you can receive Radio Maitai. Toto, the only paid employee of the station, acts also as de facto director of the small research library housed in the *mairie*. The church housing the station has been reclaimed so it will have to move when it gets permanent quarters.

Walk east for another 100 yards or so and the pink boulangerie is on your left. The only evidence that the structure is a bakery is the existence of three 7-inch metal stacks

exiting the building, two horizontally in the front and another through the roof. Be sure to get to the boulangerie before 10 a.m. because they will run out of bread after that.

Next to the boulangerie is a hamburger stand called **Snack Stella**. Here's the deal. All and all, it's not too bad. The hamburger buns are made from the same French bread dough as the baguettes and are therefore a bit chewy. The trick is to bite through the sandwich without squirting the meat morsel out the other end. Practice makes perfect.

A wood carver's shop located above the hamburger stand houses pieces by true artisans. It is worth a trip just to see the work if not to buy a piece or two.

Next, down the street on the same side is a small hotel/restaurant called **Moana Nui** ("great big ocean" in Marquesan), known mostly for its wood-fired brick pizza oven. Their most famous pizza is one in which they plop a fried egg into the center. The pizza is excellent, though I have never been able to handle an egg looking up at me from my pizza.

Continuing east a few yards is an institution on Nuku Hiva, **Magasin Maurice**. Maurice McKittrick's father, Bob, started the store when Maurice was a young man. He was here when Sterling Hayden rolled in on *Wanderer* in the late 1950s and only recently has enlarged the store. Maurice carries groceries, canned goods, frozen meat and cool drinks—including beer. He does not sell bread, but more important, he sells fuel. Bring in your jerry cans and he will fill them for you with diesel or gas. (They will fill your propane tanks here also, though I prefer to fill mine at Magasin Bigot.) If your purchases are large and difficult to carry, Adeline, a pretty Marquesan will gladly drive you and your load back to the beach.

I take personal responsibility for the cruddy yellowish color of Maurice's shop. I was walking by just before the new store opened while the undercoat was being applied to the outside. Maurice, in his inimitable accent asked me, "Hey, what color you think good for store?" He sounds like a falsetto Tonto. I told him bright yellow would be great as the boats could use the store as a range marker from far out to sea; maybe even from Ua Pou!

"Good idea," he replied. He went over to the painter and instructed him to put in the yellow tint. The next day I came back to find the building painted its current sick yellow. I asked Maurice what happened. He said, "I know it's not so yellow but I don't have so much yellow tint. Only two tubes." *C'est la vie.*

If you need a large fuel order, send a fax to Maurice at (689) 920-391. (He has a sophisticated fax system: call first, tell him you want to fax, then he will hook up the fax to the same number.)

Across the street and diagonally from Magasin Maurice is a building that houses both the marché (meat and vegetable market) and **Boutique Kanahau**. The clothing sold here is of good quality and priced accordingly. The marché has a good supply of fresh and frozen meat and fresh produce. The best day to hit the marché is early Friday when produce is delivered from Siki's garden in Taipivai. (Siki's garden is more like a small truck farm; he grows lettuce, cucumbers, cabbage, squash, grapefruit, taro and tomatoes.)

Across from the marché, in the "V" of the confluence of the airport and strand roads, is **Magasin Larson** which used to be called Magasin François after it original owner, a delightful Chinese gentleman who now lives in Tahiti. Françcois has turned over the management of the store to his son-in-law, Larson, thus the name change. The store has general merchandise and groceries as does Maurice's but Larson's also has a good supply of outboard motor accessories and fishing gear that differentiates the two stores. Baguettes are also sold here and you may be able to buy a few after the boulangerie has run out. Magasin Larson is open from 6:30 to 11:30 a.m. and 1:30 to 5 p.m., Monday through Saturday.

Last, but certainly not least on the list of markets, is **Magasin Kamake**, owned and operated by the Leau Choy family headed by patriarch Kamake Leau Choy, a former mayor of Taiohae. With his wife Mareta and a multitude of children, children-in-law and grandchildren, Kamake has been providing groceries to the community for years. The modern bakery behind the store bakes several hundred baguettes per day and the crust is a little more crisp than that at the boulangerie. (I like the crispy crust so I buy my bread here.) One daughter, Marie-Hélène, is an expert chef and between duty with Air Tahiti, bakes and decorates cakes along with cooking Chinese, French and Marquesan food for the family meals. With a day or two notice, she will prepare magnificent birthday cakes and special food orders.

Marie-Hélène's significant other, Fred, is a mechanic par excellence who specializes in refrigeration repair. Though he now works at the Post Office, he can point you in the right direction for refrigerator repair. (Freon 12 and 22 are available at Kamake's.) Fred originally arrived in the archipelago aboard a French navy survey ship, met Marie-Hélène, and the rest is history.

Maurice Leau Choy and his wife Marie-Louise Gendron Leau Choy (Marie-Louise is a cousin of Bruno Gendron of Nuku Hiva Village) work hard to keep Magasin Kamake stocked with the goods most Marquesans and cruisers want. If there is anything you need but cannot find on Nuku Hiva, Marie-Louise or Maurice can find it for you. Marie-Louise speaks English and has been assisting visiting yachtsmen for years.

Magasin Kamake
Phone: (689) 920-322
Fax: (689) 920-341
Visa and MasterCard are welcome.

Hours: 7 - 11:30 a.m. and 2 - 5:30 p.m.

Continue walking east down the strand to find the bank. Banque Socredo is on the left behind four huge *Kiglia Pinnata* (Sausage) trees. Newly renovated, this bank offers worldwide banking services including cash advances on credit cards. There is currently a limit of U.S. $350 per week on credit card advances.

Farther down on the same side of the street is the *mairie*, the local government offices. Just past the mairie there is a small shopping plaza housing a travel agency, boutique, hair salon, and a dentist's office. The **Shop Loisirs**, in the same plaza, makes copies, sells souvenirs, stamps, film, camera batteries, post cards, etc. Beyond the shops there is open ground where the food *barraques* (stalls) are erected during fête each July.

A few more yards east finds you at the road that leads to the old dock. Although it's farther from your boat, if you tie your dinghy up here, you could do this walk in reverse and be closer to town. Plan to get to the quay at about 6:30 a.m. on most days where you can buy fresh tuna, mahi and wahoo at very reasonable prices. That's the good news. The bad news is you usually have to buy the whole fish which might weigh 50 kilos or more. You might want to get together with another cruiser or two and split up the meat. Jean-Marie Robert, the diminutive ex-chef at Keikehanui Inn, taught me the most efficient way to turn a 20- or 30-kilo tuna into steaks and fillets. He could do it in 10 minutes without wasting an ounce.

Ha'e and sculpture at shore -front park, Taiohae

Leaving the old dock, walk back up the hill. About 100 yards back up the main road you come to a fork in the road where you will find the post office. One of Kamake's sons, Christian, works in the post office and speaks English well. He and Fred, can take care of placing your phone calls back home.

The road to the left passes by the gendarmerie; the one on the right leads to the hospital. One of the fine doctors at the hospital working under Chief of Staff, Odile Simoné, is Phillip Vaysse who arrived aboard his 32-foot aluminum cutter *Virus* after years of cruising. The hospital is well staffed and supplies free anti-filariosis tablets. *Filariosis* is a disease—spread by a mosquito—that causes the extremities to swell to elephantine proportions, hence its name, *elephantiasis*. Though only one bite is necessary for infection, it is rare, so doctors do not recommend taking the pills if you are planning to stay less than 4 or 5 months. I took no chances and gobbled a pill in the first week after arrival.

Now that you have mailed the backlog of letters and cards to the folks and cured your filariosis, it is time to go to the gendarmerie and get legal. Head eastward up the hill from the post office on the left. The process is painless and the officers are all friendly with a good sense of humor.

**Magasin Bigot** (*beeg-oh*) has some hardware not available anywhere else on the island—notably, a small supply of stainless nuts, bolts and screws. The problem is getting there. It is a mile up the inland road from Magasin François on the left over a small bridge, and is hard to see from the road. However, it's the best place to get your propane bottles filled. They managed to get more gas into my tanks than anyone could in the States. Bigot will give you a lift back to your dinghy when you have finished your shopping.

Magasin Bigot
Phone: 920-434

# Chief Pakoko, *the uncooperative Marquesan*

The first *hao'e* (white man) to discover Nuku Hiva was American naval Captain Duncan Ingraham in 1791 who named it Federal Island.

The island enjoyed relative peace until 1842, when the French annexed the Marquesas and established a garrison in Taiohae. There was preliminary resistance by several chiefs on Nuku Hiva, but by 1845 a tenuous rapport was reached between the French battalion commander, named Almeric, and the most influential chief in Taiohae, Temoana (*temoana* means, "the ocean" in Marquesan).

Temoana was pro-French, and together he and Almeric issued a joint regulation making the bay and its environs *tapu* (out of bounds) for women due to Almeric's disapproval of the nightly orgies taking place near the beach at Taiohae. Native women were also commuting out to the French navy ships anchored in the harbor.

Smoldering in the background was another Taiohae chief, Pakoko who, although he had refused to accept French domination, up to now had shown no propensity for violence. Pakoko protested the new *tapu* on behalf of his tribe. The women rallied to his defense but 26 females were caught *in flagrante dilicto* in defiance of the regulation. They were sentenced to 48 hours in the jail, which, for a Marquesan, is an unbearable personal humiliation. To add to the problem, two of the prisoners were Pakoko's daughters.

Pakoko was outraged and called his warriors to avenge the insult. Within a few days, six French soldiers were killed in an ambush. The French mounted hunting parties and finally captured Pakoko. A hastily arranged trial condemned him to be shot. As he was led to the wall, it is told that he calmly stated, "I washed the prison dust from my daughter with French blood." He refused a blindfold and was killed by six bullets.

The unfortunate circumstances of Pakoko's death started general discontent within the Nuku Hiva population and the French were forced to call a great "koika" or meeting of chiefs. This meeting was successful and renewed the tribal relationships with the French.

The six dead French sailors are buried beneath the monument next to the marché without any acknowledgment of their demise at the site. The monument is unnamed but it has a flag, a cannon, and a short inscription in commemoration of the annexation of the islands.

Commemorative monument, Taiohae

## TAIOA BAY
### HAKATEA ("DANIEL'S BAY") & HAKAUI

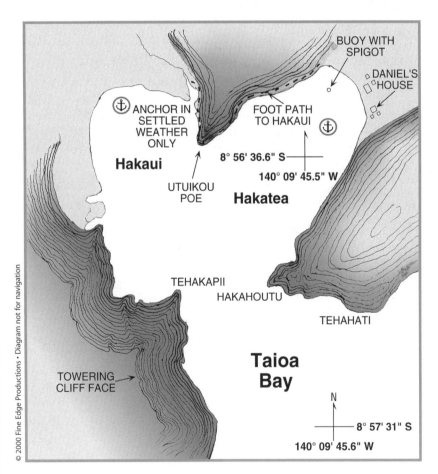

BUOY WITH SPIGOT

DANIEL'S HOUSE

ANCHOR IN SETTLED WEATHER ONLY

FOOT PATH TO HAKAUI

Hakaui

8° 56' 36.6" S

140° 09' 45.5" W

UTUIKOU POE

Hakatea

TEHAKAPII

HAKAHOUTU

TEHAHATI

Taioa Bay

N

8° 57' 31" S

140° 09' 45.6" W

TOWERING CLIFF FACE

© 2000 Fine Edge Productions • Diagram not for navigation

One of the most well-known destinations outside Taiohae on Nuku Hiva is Baie Taioa. Baie Taioa contains two coves: Hakaui and Hakatea. To find Taioa from Taiohae, slide west down the south coast of Nuku Hiva until your G.P.S. longitude reads 140°09'45.8". Then, look right NNE! The cliffs are dramatic sentinels to this lovely bay. Those same cliffs form the western terminus of Taohae's outer volcanic crater that arcs eastward ending dramatically at Point Tikapo near Taipivai.

The first beach you see is at Hakaui and after you take Hakahoutu Point to starboard, you have a full view of Hakatea on the same side. Again, there are no unseen obstructions into either bay. Hakatea is usually less rolly than Hakaui. However, in unsettled easterly or southeasterly weather, Hakaui is unusable and even Hakatea is rolly enough to demand the use of a stern anchor to hold your bow toward the beach. This roll comes from a wave "echo" off the cliffs to the west.

### ⚓ ANCHORING TIPS

**Hakatea:** Other than the possiblity of needing a stern anchor if southeasterly seas are bouncing off the western cliffs, Hakatea is the better of the two anchor sites. Anchor clear of the water buoys closer to shore. The bottom has good holding in 25-35 feet.

**Hakaui:** Although Hakatea is your best bet, Hakaui can be a "lake" in settled northerly weather. There are no obstructions while entering Hakaui and anchoring is firm 3 to 5 fathoms with a sand bottom.

### 🛶 GOING ASHORE

The shore at Hakatea is a nice, sandy beach. On the north end it leads to the ancient path over to Hakaui; the south end terminates at Daniel's house (see below). You can land a dinghy anywhere along the beach in settled weather but during southeasterly weather it is easier to land near the house on the south end of the beach.

# HAKATEA

*(Hah-kah-tay-ah)*

Hakatea has been given the name "Daniel's Bay" by American cruisers simply because Kremont Teiketohe de Daniel (aka Daniel) has lived and welcomed cruisers there for many years. While he is not comfortable with the name "Daniel's Bay," he accepts it with grace.

From the anchorage looking west, you will see a most impressive series of cliffs. The three tallest peaks starting from seaward are: Tavaitimaka; Moopa, just north of Point Utukoupoe; and the tallest, Taopoka in Hakaui Valley. On the other side of these cliffs is arid land sloping gently westward toward the sea called Terre Dessert (Desert Land) by the French and Henua Taha (Land for Walking) by the Marquesans.

There are currently four buoys set in Hakatea. The northwestern-most has a water spigot sticking through the middle of it which is attached to a black, flexible polypropylene water pipe leading from the shore. These buoys and the water service were installed by Daniel. It is a very handy service that Daniel and his wife Heiani (Antoinette is her French name) offer in Hakatea. For those of us who do not enjoy the luxury of a water maker, being able to pull up to a water hose and fill the tanks saves hours of schlepping

Hakatea, author sketch

jerry cans from shore to boat. As a courtesy, go ashore to meet Daniel before taking on water. He will give you anchoring instructions so that you do not inadvertently pick up the water line running along the bottom toward shore. In some conditions fore and aft anchoring may be necessary while you take on water. Under all circumstances, you *must* use your own anchor while taking on water. The ground tackle for the buoy holding the spigot is not designed to hold a boat. Furthermore, there is no pennant to which you can attach your boat. Remember, Daniel has installed this pipe as a friendly gesture to yachtsmen; he has no ulterior motive and makes no money from the yachts. He asks that the water be used only for filling tanks and not for washdown.

A font of information on the history and legends of the Marquesas, Daniel enjoys talking to yachties and will ask you to sign his guestbook. His Marquessan name, Teiketohe, means "Persistent Prince." He laughs and slaps a knee when he knows you understand the meaning. Antoinette's Marquesan name, Heiani, means "Flower Wreath from the Sky." (*Hei* = Wreath [*lei* in Hawaiian], *Ani* = Sky.) The Marquesans really know the good names for their kids!

North of Daniel's house there are several abandoned structures. This "complex" was built by a local entrepreneur as a funky bar/restaurant for cruisers. The operator is reported to be ill and there has been no service for some time.

# HAKAUI

*(hah-kah-wee)*

Simeon and René Kimitete live near the beach at Hakaui. Lucas, a full-bearded relative of Daniel, lives there also and helps with copra harvest. The supply ship *Aranui* occasionally visits the bay to pick up copra and let its passengers hike to Vaipo, one of the most spectacular waterfalls in the world.

The 1,800-meter walk to Vaipo—a popular sight in the Marquesas—starts in the center of the beach at Hakaui. The trek generally follows the river and can be gruelling especially if it has been raining. But if you take the hike, you will be rewarded with a free-fall cascade of over 900 feet (300+ meters). (This was measured by Yves Cousteau in a helicopter several years ago.) The refreshing pool at the bottom, called Hauii, is *cold!*

# BAIE DU CONTRÔLEUR
## HAKAPAA, KAPUVAI & HANGA HAA

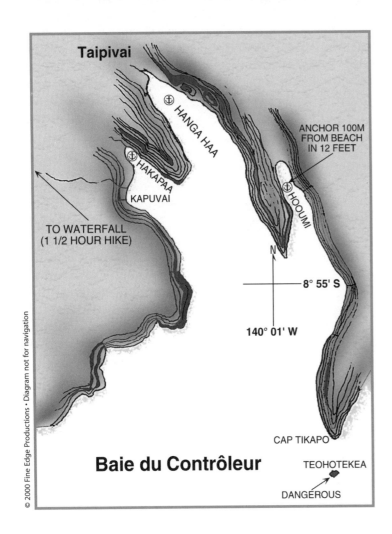

Taipivai

HANGA HAA

HAKAPAA

KAPUVAI

TO WATERFALL
(1 1/2 HOUR HIKE)

ANCHOR 100M
FROM BEACH
IN 12 FEET

HOOUMI

N

8° 55' S

140° 01' W

CAP TIKAPO

Baie du Contrôleur

TEOHOTEKEA

DANGEROUS

© 2000 Fine Edge Productions · Diagram not for navigation

At the southeast corner of Nuku Hiva, Baie du Contrôleur has four separate sections. From west to east: Kapuvai and Hakapaa share a common cove to the west; Hanga Haa is the bay in front of Taipivai; Hooumi is the pinky finger lying to the east. Baie du Contrôleur on the windward part of the island is always verdant and humid. The green cliffs along shore give a more tropical feel than the drier, western sections.

## ⚓ ANCHORING TIPS

**Hakapaa and Kapuvai:** It is best to anchor in Hakappa in 25 feet of sandy mud and dinghy to Kapuvai for a hike to a waterfall that is well worth the hour-and-a-half trek. Although Kapuvai is not a particularly comfortable anchorage, it is closer to the waterfall. There are a lot of urchins and octopi in Kakapaa and Kapuvai if that strikes your fancy.

**Hanga Haa:** The bottom comes up regularly as you approach the beach at Taipivai (Hanga Haa) until you reach a depth of 12 feet when it levels out and stays at 12-18 feet until about 100 yards from shore. The bottom has sandy mud and holds well. Little or no swell enters the bay so fore and aft anchoring is not usually necessary.

## 🛶 GOING ASHORE

**Hanga Haa:** Facing the sand, you will see a hut on the left (west) end of the beach. On the right (east), there are small tidal breakers at the mouth of the river that flows from the valley. At high tide, you can row your dinghy up the river all the way to the village where there is a concrete dock and a block building a few hundred yards up river. However, if you prolong your visit, your dinghy will be trapped until the next high tide. For an extended visit to the village it is better to leave your dinghy on the west end of the beach where a road follows the west side of the valley and leads to Siki's house and garden. Or, you can beach your dink on the west end of the beach, walk to the east end, ford the river and walk north down the road to the village.

# Walking tour: Taipivai

Hanga Haa is most famous for its location at the foot of Taipivai (*Tai-pee-vai*). Taipivai is the valley where Herman Melville hid after jumping ship in Taiohae. He and a shipmate, Richard Tobias (Toby) Greene, slipped away from the whaler *Acushnet* while on shore duty. According to Melville, the captain was a tyrant and they couldn't take his abuse any longer. So they fled, avoiding the search parties and ending up in the valley of the "Typee." The story—whether true or not—gives a general idea of the ancient Marquesan life style. The most startling aspect of the book is the difference in population; Taipivai which had thousands of inhabitants during Melville's two-month visit now has barely 300 living in the valley.

After a mile, the road up the western side of the valley turns right and crosses the river. Another right and a few hundred yards back toward the bay, you will be at the block building across the street from **Magasin Haiti** (*hah-ee-tee*). Remember that you need the correct adapters to buy some propane through Magasin Haiti. Another shop, **Magasin Cécile**, is north of the bridge and carries the same basic items as Magasin Haiti.

There is no fuel available here. (In a pinch, a friendly Marquesan might sell you a gallon or two to get you back to Taiohae.)

A *tiki* and some *paepaes* are located within an hour's hike from the village. Tracey Smith Tavira, who lives in Taiohae, says it is an "easy walk," but she's an aerobics instructor. Most of the people I have talked to say the trail to the *tiki* is a "death march" and not worth the trouble. Others were struck by a sense of history when they viewed the ancient relics that were no doubt seen by Melville.

I hope you enjoy this historic, beautiful, tropical paradise. But my favorite is yet to come.

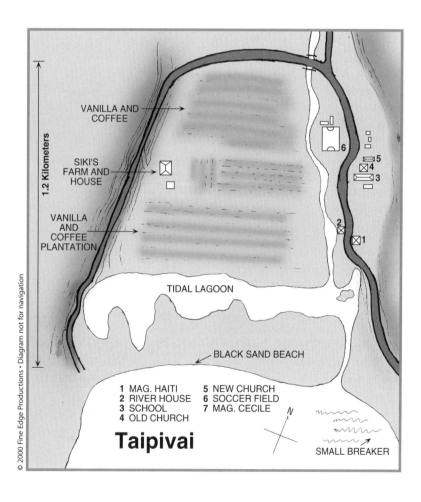

VANILLA AND COFFEE

SIKI'S FARM AND HOUSE

VANILLA AND COFFEE PLANTATION

1.2 Kilometers

TIDAL LAGOON

BLACK SAND BEACH

1 MAG. HAITI
2 RIVER HOUSE
3 SCHOOL
4 OLD CHURCH
5 NEW CHURCH
6 SOCCER FIELD
7 MAG. CECILE

**Taipivai**

SMALL BREAKER

## Herman Melville

Herman Melville was only 13 when his father, Allen Melvill (the 'e' was added later) died in 1832. He had to quit school and, although he tried to follow in his brother Gansevoort's financial footsteps, he did not succeed. At age 19—following the economic crash of 1837 that caused many young men to gravitate toward seafaring—he signed aboard a trading ship as cabin boy. He made one round trip to England and returned to New York with little to show for his trouble.

He shuffled around New York and New England for several years and finally signed aboard a new whaling ship, the *Acushnet.* The whaling industry which was faring better than the rest of the economy continued to do so throughout the Civil War years. Melville's mother, considered that the seafaring occupations were for those without other practical aptitudes, and she was not happy about her son's offshore pursuits. Nevertheless, in 1841 Herman was off on a whaling adventure "under a spread of sail."

In this golden age of whaling, the crew were paid only a small percentage of the take, so whalers remained at sea until the holds were filled, insuring financial success for the voyage. After 18 months and the prospect of more years at sea, the blush wore off the rose. The *Acushnet* could not find whales and the hold was far from full. Moreover, the captain was a despotic, raving tyrant in Melville's eyes, and jumping ship began to seem a viable alternative.

By the time *Acushnet* arrived in Taiohae, Nuku Hiva, Melville had found a kindred spirit in Tobias (Toby) Greene—a fellow seaman aboard the whaler. Toby was also inclined to abandon ship, and after some quick planning that included squirreling away some food, the two men sneaked off the ship and up into the highlands above the bay. *Acushnet's* captain offered a reward for their capture but, after a few weeks, he gave up the search and sailed off.

The two deserters hiked overland and scrambled down the steep cliffs that protect the Taipi valley on the southeast corner of the island. Though all Marquesan tribes practiced cannibalism at the time, the people of Taipi were known as the cannibal's cannibals. Stories of the cannibalistic rituals of the Taipi were uppermost in the men's minds as they climbed down through the jungle canopy and lava-rock boulders. During the descent, Melville hurt his leg and, by the time they reached the valley floor, he was nearly immobile.

River at Taipivai

Taipivai, author sketch

The Taipi surprised the men with their generous care of Melville's leg, but the two men were still suspicious of the Marquesans' motives. When an opportunity to leave arose, Toby left ostensibly to find help for Herman. He never returned, and Melville found himself alone as the guest of the savages, not knowing whether he was being prepared as a side dish for this infamous tribe. After a few weeks, he decided to make a run for it and managed to find his way out of the valley and back to Taiohae.

Melville signed aboard the Australian whaler, *Lucy Ann*, only to find that she was more ill-found than *Acushnet*. A week later, as soon as *Lucy Ann* reached Tahiti, he joined another group of mutineers and was thrown into Papeete's rattan jailhouse. This was hardly solitary confinement for he was allowed to wander around Papeete most of the time. After a couple more years of South Seas escapades that also took him to Hawaii, Melville reached Boston in 1844, nearly four years after shipping out on *Acushnet*. He would never see the South Seas again.

As soon as he returned home, he wrote a book about his Taipi adventure. Although the story was compared favorably to Daniel Defoe's yarn about Alexander Selkirk, New York publishers passed on the manuscript declaring it "impossible that it could be true." Herman's brother, Gansevoort—in London at the time—helped him find an English publisher for *Typee* who simultaneously published the book in America. Melville followed up with a sequel, *Omoo* (which means "wanderer"), about his time in Tahiti's jail. However, reviewers again doubted the credibility of his story, thinking it unlikely that a deckhand could write so well, and openly accusing him of fabricating the entire story of the Taipi. His publisher wanted proof of of the adventure, which Herman assured him was "a little touched up . . . but true." If it was true, then where was Toby? Where indeed?

Richard Tobias Greene happened to be working as a housepainter in Buffalo, New York, when he read the reviews by the doubting Thomases. In hopes that Melville would see them, he wrote letters to the newspapers declaring himself the real Toby of Typee. Herman did see the letters and he traveled to Buffalo to confirm Greene's identity and find out why his friend had abandoned him to the fate of the savages. Greene claimed that he had been pressed aboard another whaler and forced to leave. Satisfied with that story, Herman sent a photo and other evidence to his publisher that Toby was real. "Truth is stranger than fiction" was heard throughout the English-speaking world.

Melville went on to write *Mardi*, *White Jacket* and his masterpiece, *Moby Dick* (1851). His novel, *Pierre*, published in 1852 was dark and psychological, and he was openly accused of being crazy. Years passed with little to note from this once-fertile mind, and he died in 1891 without fanfare. The New York Times' obituary misspelled his name, but the plaque on the beach in Taiohae spells the name of one of the Marquesas' most distiguished visitors correctly while commemorating his short time on the island.

# ANAHO BAY

In my personal opinion, Anaho Bay is the finest anchorage in French Polynesia. Whether you leave from Taiohae or Taipivai, you round Cap Tikapi, on the southeast corner of Nuku Hiva, and head north to Cap Matauaoa. Rounding Cap Tikapi needs a bit of attention. A half-mile south of the point is a "jumping" rock called Teohootekea. In bad weather, the rock can be difficult to see, so beware. Pass it to seaward.

The trip up the east coast of Nuku Hiva is spectacular in its ruggedness. If you stay within a mile of the shore, you will be rewarded with a dolphin show Sea World would be proud of. After rounding Matauaoa, don't turn into Haahaivea before Anaho. Motu Poiku can be mistaken for tiny Muto Iti which guards the eastern entrance to Anaho. Head for the western side of the bay and round the headland (Matoohotu).

## ⚓ ANCHORING TIPS

Tuck the boat into the lee of Matoohotu and anchor in 12 to 20 feet of sand and coral. Don't worry, you'll get used to hearing your anchor chain grind on the coral heads. During a lengthy stay, you may wrap the rode around a coral head or two making your departure a bit more complicated than you expected.

## 🚣 GOING ASHORE

The beach is the only dinghy landing and a hole in the reef is the only safe passage to the beach. Two sets of buoys mark the channel. Two sets of buoys mark the seaward opening; the buoys closer to the beach are used also to moor fishing boats. Don't deviate from a line between the two sets of buoys because you will nail your dinghy prop even at high tide. The beach by the creek outflow is the obvious dinghy landing. If you haul your dinghy up on shore, you may find it 50 feet from the water when you return due to ebb tide, so it is best to leave it offshore using a dinghy anchor. The water shallows gently here so you never have to swim for your dink.

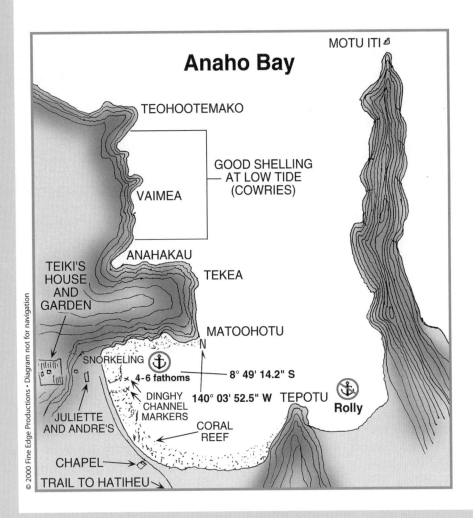

Anaho Bay

MOTU ITI

TEOHOOTEMAKO

GOOD SHELLING AT LOW TIDE (COWRIES)

VAIMEA

ANAHAKAU

TEIKI'S HOUSE AND GARDEN

TEKEA

MATOOHOTU

SNORKELING

8° 49' 14.2" S

4-6 fathoms

140° 03' 52.5" W   TEPOTU

DINGHY CHANNEL MARKERS

Rolly

JULIETTE AND ANDRE'S

CORAL REEF

CHAPEL

TRAIL TO HATIHEU

© 2000 Fine Edge Productions · Diagram not for navigation

# Anaho

*(ah-nah-ho)*

I hope you enjoy and appreciate Anaho as much as I do. The resident Vaiaanui family here are among my dearest friends. André and Juliette Vaiaanui, with sons Leopold and Teiki, collect six tons of copra per month from the coco palms covering the hillsides of Anaho. Before the world-wide collapse of tropical oil prices, 20 men worked the plantation. Now the French government offers price subsidies to copra workers and only family members work here now.

Juliette is an aunt of Bruno Gendron at Nuku Hiva Village and Marie-Louise Leau Choy at Magasin Hoata in Taiohae. She and André also run a small pension out of their home.

Teiki used to grow veggies for sale in Haiheu and Taiohae, but they have built some new bungalows and now limit their business to copra and the pension.

The fresh water is sweet at Anaho. Teiki built the water supply from a spring near Haatuatua to the east. One high spigot is near the line of ironwood trees on the beach. A clothes-line is normally strung between the trees as it is a favorite spot for doing laundry, taking showers, and filling jerry jugs. Behind the main house, there is a pit for garbage disposal. A sign directs you to the *poubelle* (garbage).

A trail behind the ironwoods leads south past a small chapel to a copra storage shed then to a huge *ficus lyrata* (fiddle leaf fig). The trail leads under the tree where there is an ancient *paepae,* then on up the slope and over the mountain to Hatiheu. The hike up to the pass takes about an hour and to continue on to Hatiheu takes another hour. The view is spectacular, so take along your camera. (Again, superwoman Tracey Smith Tavira, says, "I do the trip in 45 minutes! *She* does, but mere mortals may take longer.)

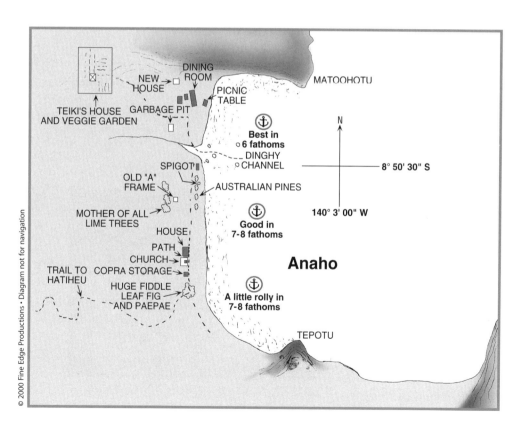

Check the anchoring map for the best place to snorkel. From Matoohutu to the northern-most dinghy channel marker, it is reminiscent of Caribbean reef snorkeling with grottos and bright tropical fish everywhere.

Juliette has set up a picnic table on the beach in front of the house. She also installed a light bulb there and, if you ask, she may leave the light on for a few hours after dark for a beach *kaikai*. We start our beach potlucks after sunset to outfox the NoNos. It is polite to buy a few Hinanos or some veggies before asking permission to use the table, as the electricity is supplied by an old Lister diesel banging away behind Teiki's house on the hill. When they keep it on, they cannot sleep so it is a true favor when they supply the lighting past their normal bedtime of 7 to 8 p.m..

## Marquesan Hospitality

One Friday night we planned a going-away *kaikai* on the beach at Taiohae for Mike and Morey, crew of *Goatlocker*. They were leaving the next day for points west. Rose at Keikehanui Inn was convinced we scheduled it to ruin her Friday night business. (Maybe she was right.) At any rate, we arranged for pigs and goats to be cooked, and Bruno at Nuku Hiva Village loaned us one of the big barbecues he uses during major events. The crews of most of the 20 boats in the anchorage had coasted by the *Christina* to ask if it was an open pot-luck, which it was. It promised to be a memorable evening. However, a few hours before the festivities began, the rain started; not some sissy drizzle, no. Big, four-pound tropical water balloons pounded the beach like D-Day. As it grew dark, the only alternative was to transfer the kaikai to the large, traditional "ha'e" up the road by the old Magasin Hoata. Justin and Julienne had been invited to the soirée so I slogged to his house behind the beach just west of the cemetery. I wanted to ask Justin who I should talk to for permission to use the "ha'e." As I slipped and slid up his sodden driveway, I noticed their patio was lit. I had a flashlight and made my way through his pamplemouse orchard to the veranda. Two 12' tables, end to end, were erected and covered with cloths, decorated with flowers and silverware was set out. Justin (pronounced joos-tahn) was tending a barbeque glowing in the corner. I asked him what was up. He patiently explained to me that since it was raining, there was no possible way our kaikai could be held on the beach so he had made provisions to hold it at his house. Fifty cruisers arrived at Justin's house that night. He knew only two of them. So goes Marquesan hospitality and friendship.

Justin and Julienne

# Hatiheu

*(hah-tee-hey-oo)*

I have spent only one night anchored in Hatiheu and that was one night too many. The anchorage is rolly under most circumstances and the wind swirls making fore and aft anchoring necessary. I recommend that you anchor in Anaho and either hike over the hill or—if you have a substantial dinghy—motor around to Hatiheu. But if you insist on anchoring at Hatiheu, there are no obstructions and the eastern side of the bay affords a bit more protection and puts you closer to the concrete dock where you can tie up your dinghy.

Walking along the strand, you will find the post office and mairie on the corner of the path to Anaho. As you travel west, the mayor of Hatiheu, Yvonne, owns the little restaurant and curio shop next to Moi Tamarii's boutique. After the church and soccer field, you cross another bridge before arriving at the road to Taiohae. Up this road are the sites of ancient paepae and tikis. A newly discovered ancient site is currently being excavated a bit further on up the road. Remember, the tiki that gave Ozanne Rohi on Hiva Oa so much trouble was found here in Hatiheu.

Hatiheu

# Pua

(poo-ah)

Pua approach

The north coast of Nuku Hiva is a treasure of gunkholing opportunities. One of the best overnight possibilities is in the bay of Hakaaehu (*Hah-kah-ah-eh-hoo*). The black sand beach at Pua is chock full of NoNos, so come prepared.

The *tapu* valley of Pua fronts the bay. Pua is known as the Valley of the Chiefs and it is *tapu* for anyone not born there to visit the valley. Of the many chiefs born there, one was the famous tattooed warrior Keikahanui. A copra plantation there is worked by Germain and Charles who are always pleased to show you around. They are hunters also and can sometimes supply you with a little fresh goat or pork if you have bartering goods.

**Making tapa, author sketch**

Tapa is the ubiquitous South Seas hand craft made by pounding bark into a coarse cloth and decorated with native motifs.

**Copra plantation at Pua**

Coconut meat is harvested and dried for export.

# Chapter 11
## EIAO

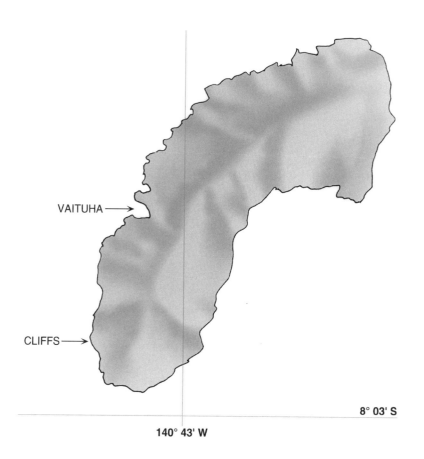

VAITUHA →

CLIFFS →

8° 03' S

140° 43' W

Sixty miles north of Nuku Hiva lies the rugged crescent-shaped island of Eiao (*Ay-ee-ow*). Except for the western end of Hiva Oa formed by the ancient volcano at Taaoa, Eiao—along with neighboring Hatutaa, aka Hatutu—is the oldest island in the group. It is uninhabited, wild, and relatively desolate.

Eiao (usually called *a-e-i-o-u* by new arrivals) is one of the few islands where the best anchorage is not a segment of a volcanic crater. The remains of the Eiao crater is on the windward side and is completely unprotected. This island is not the dream destination for all cruisers. If, however, you enjoy lonely, windswept, desolate nature preserves, Eiao is paradise.

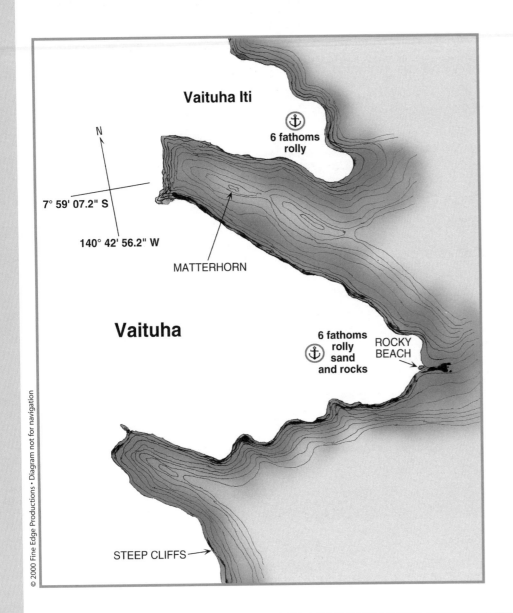

Vaituha Iti

N

7° 59' 07.2" S

140° 42' 56.2" W

MATTERHORN

Vaituha

6 fathoms
rolly

6 fathoms
rolly
sand
and rocks

ROCKY
BEACH

STEEP CLIFFS

© 2000 Fine Edge Productions • Diagram not for navigation

# VAITUHA

Leave Anaho Bay on the north coast of Nuku Hiva at sundown, and you should fetch Eiao at about sun-up. Those of you who cruise in maxis will have a much shorter voyage.

There are two anchorages: Vaituha is half-way up the western coast, and "next door," to the north, is Vaituha Iti. (This is not the official name of the Vaituha Ita but I could not find a chart or a person indicating its real name.)

Sailing along the west coast of Eiao is one of the highlights of a trip to this small island. The spectacular cliffs are loaded with bird life and dolphins gambol alongside the boat. From south to north, the first obvious recession of the cliffs marks the southern entrance to Vaituha. Do not confuse Vaituha with Vaitahu on Tahuata as one chart does.

## ⚓ ANCHORING TIPS

The Vaituha is not the best anchorage in the Marquesas. Stay centered in the bay. Fore and aft anchoring will be necessary unless the weather is really boring and flat. It is deep (60 to 90 feet) and usually quite rolly. The bottom is rocky and it can take a few tries before the hook is secure.

## 🚣 GOING ASHORE

So far I've really made this place alluring. But wait, the worst is yet to come. At the head of the bay is a steep, stony beach. The obvious landing point is to the right where a stream meets the sea. Getting ashore can be an exciting event. Unless the anchorage is flat, don't try going ashore. More people have pitchpoled their dinghies here than anywhere else in the Marquesas. Some have found the rocky beach makes for a more difficult departure than landing.

# Eiao

Once safely ashore, the rugged landscape is daunting but with perseverance, you may climb to enjoy some magnificent views of Hatutu, Motu One, and in clear weather, Nuku Hiva 60 miles to the south. You can see sheep and goats on Eiao; hunting expeditions from Nuku Hiva arrive regularly to cull the herds. You, of course, are not allowed to hunt anywhere in the archipelago. The rocks bordering Vaituha are full of lobsters for you night divers and fish (including hammerhead sharks) abound.

A new archeological dig on Eiao yields evidence that the ancient Marquesans made regular visits to the little island to bring back a type of rock that was useful in making their adzes and other tools.

Eiao was once considered for the honor of being ground zero for France's Pacific atomic bomb testing program. Eiao's gain was Mururoa's loss. That unfortunate atoll in the Tuamotu will spend the next few million years recovering from environmental annihilation.

# Appendixes

### The Legend of Fire

In ancient times it is said that the people of Fenua Enata ate only cold food. They had no fire and the raw food tasted bad. However, fire was possessed only by old Mahuike, who dined grandly on cooked meat. The people of Fenua Enata requested that Mahuike's grandson, Maui, ask the old man for fire. Maui agreed and went to see his grandfather. Mahuike did not want to give his fire away but finally touched a stick to his foot and fire started smoldering on the stick. Maui walked away with the flames. As soon as he was out of sight, he put the fire out in a stream and walked back to Mahuike. "The fire went out, Grandfather", said Maui. The old man was angered. "Please give me fire again," pleaded Maui. The old man relented and touched his knee with the stick and it burst into flames.

Maui once again dowsed the flame and returned to Mahuike. This time the grandfather refused and roared with anger. "Then I must fight you for the fire!" replied Maui. A great battle raged but finally Maui, being the younger, prevailed when Mahuike struck his head on a rock. His head hit with such force that fire was absorbed by all rocks, stones and sticks.

This is the reason that fire can be started by rubbing sticks or striking stones together.

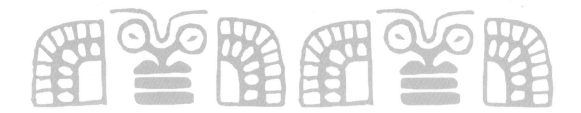

# Appendix A

# TABLE OF SERVICES

## Hiva Oa

| | ATUONA (TAAHUKU) | HANAMENU | HANAIAPA | PUA MAU |
|---|---|---|---|---|
| Port of entry | ● | | | |
| Fuel | ● | | | |
| Medical | ● | | | |
| Mcchanical (minor) | ● | | | |
| Mechanical (major) | ○[1] | | | |
| Canvas repair | ○[2] | | | |
| Food provisions | ● | | | |
| Restaurants | ● | | | |
| Phone service | ● | | | |
| Potable public water | ● | ●[3] | | |
| Garbage facilities | ● | | | |
| Showers on shore | ● | ●[4] | | |
| Archeological site | ● | | | ● |
| Waterfall (Or exceptionally nice walk) | ● | | | ● |

[1] *Major mechanical work is sometimes done by employees of the public works department or by the some of the members of the French Army brigade but **only in their spare time**. Their normal job is to rebuild and maintain the various tractors and other equipment used by the goverment.*

[2] *There are many seamstresses on the island who will be glad to help you with light sail or awning repairs.*

[3] *The spring that feeds a pond is good water.*

[4] *The pond makes a great bathtub.*

# Fatu Hiva

| | HANAVAVE |
|---|---|
| Port of entry | |
| Fuel | *Small amount (gasoline only)* |
| Medical | |
| Mechanical (minor) | |
| Mechanical (major) | |
| Canvas repair | |
| Food provisions | ● |
| Restaurants | |
| Phone service | ● |
| Potable public water | ● |
| Garbage facilities | ● |
| Showers on shore | |
| Archeological site | |
| Waterfall (or exceptionally nice walk) | ● |

# Tahuata

| | DESANIS COVE (ANSE DESANIS) | VAITAHU | IVAIVA | HANA MOE NOA |
|---|---|---|---|---|
| Port of entry | | | | |
| Fuel | | *Small amounts* | | |
| Medical | | | | |
| Mechanical (minor) | | | | |
| Mechanical (major) | | | | |
| Canvas repair | | | | |
| Food provisions | | ● | | |
| Restaurants | | *Guest Houses* | | |
| Phone service | | ● | | |
| Potable public water | ● | ● | | |
| Garbage facilities | | ● | | |
| Showers on shore | | | | |
| Archeological site | ● | | | |
| Waterfall (or exceptionally nice walk) | ● | | | |

# Ua Huka

| | HANE | VAIPAEE |
|---|---|---|
| Port of entry | | |
| Fuel | *Small amounts* | *Small amounts* |
| Medical | | |
| Mechanical (minor) | | |
| Mechanical (major) | | |
| Canvas repair | | |
| Food provisions | | |
| Restaurants | ● | ● |
| Phone service | ● | ● |
| Potable public water | ● | ● |
| Garbage facilities | ● | ● |
| Showers on shore | | |
| Archeological site | ● | |
| Waterfall (or exceptionally nice walk) | | ● |

# Ua Pou

| | HAKAHAU | HAKATEHAU | VAIEHU |
|---|---|---|---|
| Port of entry | ● | | |
| Fuel | ● | *Small amounts* | |
| Medical | ● | | |
| Mechanical (minor) | ● | | |
| Mechanical (major) | ○[1] | | |
| Canvas repair | ○[2] | | |
| Food provisions | ● | ● | |
| Restaurants | ● | *Guest Houses* | |
| Phone service | ● | ● | |
| Potable public water | ● | ● | |
| Garbage facilities | ● | ● | |
| Showers on shore | ● | | |
| Archeological site | ● | | *Nearby* |
| Waterfall ( or exceptionally nice walk) | | ● | |

[1]  *Major mechanical work is sometimes done by employees of the public works department **but only in their spare time**.*

[2]  *There are many seamstresses on the island who will be glad to help you with light sail and awning repairs*

# NUKU HIVA

| | TAIOHAE | HAKATEA | HAKAUI | TAIPIVAI (CONTROLLER BAY) | ANAHO | HATIHEU | PUA |
|---|---|---|---|---|---|---|---|
| Port of entry | ● | | | | | | |
| Fuel | ● | | | Small Amount | | Small Amount | |
| Medical | ● | | | | | | |
| Mechanical (minor) | ● | | | | | | |
| Mechanical (major) | ○[1] | | | | | | |
| Canvas repair | ○[2] | | | | | | |
| Food provisions | ● | | | ● | Guest House fare | ● | |
| Restaurants | ● | | | ● (small shop) | Guest House | ● | |
| Phone service | ● | | | ● | Private Phone | ● | |
| Potable public water | ○[3] | ●[4] | | ● | ● | ● | |
| Garbage facilities | ● | | | ● | ● | ● | |
| Showers on shore | ● | ● | | | ● | | |
| Archeological site | ● | | | ● | | ● | |
| Waterfall (or exceptionally nice walk) | | | ● | ● | ● | | |

[1]  Major mechanical work is sometimes done by employees of the public works department **but only in their spare time**. Their normal job is to rebuild and maintain the various tractors and other equipment used by the government.

[2]  A French sailmaker and upholsterer that used to service the yacht crowd left the island but will surely be replaced soon. Otherwise, there are many seamstresses on the island who will be glad to help you with minor sail repairs. Ask Mary Louise at Kamake's to point you in the right direction. Raymond Gendron's wife has my old Pfaff and, if she's up to it, she should be able to sew about anything you need.

[3]  There are spigots on the beach and at the old dock but there are so many animals in the catchment area that you shouldn't drink the water without adding some Halizone tablets or a few drops of bleach to each five gallon jerry can.

[4]  The most convenient place to fill your water tanks because the spigot is on a buoy a few yards offshore.

# EIAO

No services available on this unihabited island.

# Appendix B

# AMATEUR RADIO

Amateur (ham) radio plays an important part in the daily life of crusing boaters. Checking in with maritime nets or other cruisers during a passage brings great peace of mind.

At present, as a courtesy, any American ham licensee can receive a temporary general class license from the French government for use during a stay in French Polynesia. This "FO Zero" license is even afforded to "Novice" class operators from the States. (FO stands for French Oceania, Zero for a temporary status; the rest of your number is usually made up of your initials.) This "FO Zero" license allows a Novice to broadcast on frequencies in French Polynesia for which, by FCC regulations, he is unlicensed in the U.S. This French license can be obtained from a net controller on the Pacific Maritime Net (14.313 MHz at 0400UCT) or the telecommunications department in Papeete. You can pick up your license when you arrive in Tahiti, but you can also obtain your "FO Zero" number by phoning the Tahiti office of France Télécom when you arrive in the Marquesas.

There is only one significant restriction when it comes to ham radio use in French Polynesia. If you want to hook up a phone patch, you must be at least 12 miles offshore. No patches to the States can be made when it is reasonable to use the telephone system.

The "Coffee Klatch" has been broadcasting uninterrupted for 14 years. Les Whitely, familiar to sailors from Seattle to the Bay of Islands, New Zealand, is a beacon in the darkness for ham-equipped cruisers. His call sign is FO5GZ. On Saturdays, at the end of the Klatch, Uncle Bill—a ham operator from Hawaii—gives a synopsis of the week's news from the States. We first learned of O.J. Simpson's legal problems from this service when Voice of America (VOA) was relatively silent on the subject.

The Pacific Maritime Net is the most widely used net for cruisers. Warm up for the Net occurs at 0400 UCT which is a good time to set up phone patches.

While the Coast Guard's automated weather broadcasts from Hawaii are nice, they frequently suffer from a lack of timeliness. We were once two days into a 750-mile-long low pressure system, "enjoying" ourselves in 40-knot winds and 12-foot seas, before the automated weather station mentioned this little detail as an addendum to their normal broadcast. A better daily source for the weather is "Arnold's Net:" 1805 UCT on 8.815MHz; 2200 UCT on 13.134MHz; 0400 UCT on 14.318MHz. Arnold (ZK1DB) broadcasts from Rarotonga in the Cook Islands. Unlike the automated stations, after he has read the news, you can ask him questions; his weather report is the most reliable in the Pacific.

The following partial list of frequencies may be of interest to boaters cruising to or within the Marquesas. I have Sue and Eric vanHamersveld to thank for their help in providing this ham radio information.

# Radio Schedules

| NAME | TIME | DAY | FREQUENCY |
|------|------|-----|-----------|
| Coffee Klatch | 1800 UCT | M, W, S | +/-14.283MHz |
| Pacific Maritime Net | 0400 UCT | Daily | 14.313MHz |
| Pitcairn Net | 0000 UCT | Sunday | 21.422MHz |
| USCG Weather, Hawaii | | | |
| | 2345 UCT | Daily | 8.765MHz |
| | 0545 UCT | Daily | 8.765MHz |
| | 1145 UCT | Daily | 8.765MHz |
| | 1745 UCT | Daily | 8.765MHz |
| VOA | A.M | Daily | 6.110MHz |
| | | Daily | 7.215MHz |
| | | Daily | 9.760MHz |
| | | Daily | 15.405MHz |
| | P.M. | Daily | 7.405MHz |

# Appendix C
# THE MARQUESAN LANGUAGE

Until recently, there has been no published English/Marquesan dictionary. Grammar books are all in written foreign languages, the best being Grammaire Marquise by François Zewen published by Te Haero Tahiti. I have supplied a short glossary here, including the French where I could find a synonym.

Marquesan is the antecedent to modern Polynesian languages; Tahitian and Hawaiian are dialects of ancient Marquesan. Though 1,200 miles farther away than Tahiti, the Hawaiian language more nearly parallels Marquesan than Tahitian. While a Hawaiian says, "Aloha", a Marquesan says, "Kaoha" (*kah-oh-hah*). In the Society Islands, however, they say, "Iorana". (The saying goes that Iorana was derived from the English, "Your Honor" and is pronounced: *yo-rah-nah*. I have it from reliable sources that this is not true, but I like the story anyway!)

Obviously, the words describing things that existed before the ancient voyages took place, are similar from island group to island group. For example, a canoe paddle is the same in Hawaiian and Marquesan, "hoe" (*ho-eh*). "Hoe's," of course, were around long before the settling of the Hawaiian archipelago. On the other hand, more modern terms differ: compass, for example, is "aveia" in the Marquesas but "panana" in Hawaii. There are also letter substitutions. Often the Hawaiians change the Marquesan "T" to a "K;" an example is the Marquesan word for an adz, "to'i" which is "ko'i" in Hawaiian. These words also show the "'" (or glottal stop) which is used as a letter. Although the syllable after the glottal stop ("'") is part of the word, the first vowel after the stop is pronounced as if it were the first letter of the word. Sometimes the glottal stop is substituted for a letter, or vice versa. For example, in Hawaiian the word for house is "hale" *(hah-lay);* in Marquesan the word is "ha'e" (*hah-eh*).

As in most Polynesian languages, superlatives are indicated in two ways. One way is by repetition, as in bitter—"kava;" bitterer is "kavakava." Another way to stress a word is by adding the word "nui" (*noo-ee*). If you want to say "hello," try "kaoha nui"—you will be pleasantly surprised at the reaction of the Marquesans and, in return, will receive the invariable reply "Kaoha!" with a wide, warm smile. They appreciate any attempt, no matter how feeble, to speak their language. Remember, the Marquesans do not consider themselves Frenchmen; they are Marquesans and fiercely proud of their legends, language and history unique to Henua Enana.

# Alphabet & Spelling

The Marquesan alphabet is shorter than the 26-letter English alphabet. There are 10 consonants plus the glottal stop: F, H, K, M, N, P', R, S, T and V; there is no L. Hawaiian, which is rich in L's, has no F's, S's, R's or T's. Marquesan has no W, whereas Hawaiian has no V. But the Hawaiians pronounce the W like a V—a holdover from the days of German influence. Thus, "Wai" is water in Hawaiian and "vai" in Marquesan. (Havai'i means heaven in Marquesan.)

The usual complement of vowels are used but are pronounced the same as in Spanish. The A is "*ah*" as in "father;" E like "*eh*" as the "a" in "fate", 'I' is "*ee*" as in "feet;" O is "*oh*" (without the normal English diphthong "oh-oo);" U is pronounced "oo" as in "pool".

To add a little confusion, the southern and northern groups of the Marquesans have slight differences in vocabulary and spelling; the most obvious is the transposition of the F in the south to H in the north. "Land" is "fenua" in Vaitahu but "henua" in Hakahetau. Another example, "citizen," is "akati'a" in Hana Vave (Fatu Hiva) but "anati'a" in Hane (Ua Huka).

# Sentences

Tense is determined by particles that precede the verb.

Commands always start with the particle A:

*A he'e* = Go!

*A noho* = Sit down.

*A tiohi meitai'i* = Watch out! (literally, "look well")

*A inu* = Drink!

The commonly used verbal form is what might be referred to as the perfect tense—a completed action or a state attained—which uses the prefixes Ua and U.

*Ua he'e 'au* = I went

*Ua 'ite 'au* = I saw

*Ua koakoa ma'ua* = We (us two) are/were pleased. (Literally, "We have reached a state of being pleased.")

*Ua ite tatou i te ihepe* = We (all of us inclusive) saw the ship.

And:

*Ua ite tatou 'ia 'otou* = We saw all of you. (Note that you use "i" for noun objects but "ia" for pronouns and names.)

*Ua ite ma'ua 'ia Te iki* = We saw Te iki (Te iki is the most common Marqusan boys' name while Tahia is the most common girls' name)

*U ha'ametau 'au* = I was afraid

*Ua po* = It's night, or it was night, depending on the context.

*Ua nui* = There are many, or it's big.

*Ua 'oa* = It's long (either size or time)

Another strange kink of Marquesan verbs is that the progressive/future aspect uses the particle E:

> *E he'e atu 'au ma he ihepe Aranui* = I will leave (go away) on the ship *Aranui*.

For progressive uses, for example, "I am going frequently," "They are always praying," one also uses E, but with a demonstrative element after the verb (nei, ana and a'a—1st, 2nd, and 3rd person respectively).

> *E pure ana otou* = You (plural) are always praying.

> *E kaikai a'a te maha'i* = The boy is always eating.

> *E he'e atu a'a 'ia* = He is always going away.

> *E tiohi atu nei tatou* = We are always looking away (from us).

> *E tetau nei ma'ua i te Pipiria* = We are always reading the Bible.

You can also use E to denote an action the occurs at the same time as another:

> *E inu nei 'au i te vai, ua koakoa ite vehine tiohi* = while drinking the water I was pleased to watch the women.

There is also another aspect—the consequential—which is used when you want to express the idea that something will happen *after* something else occurs—a consequence of another action. This uses the particle "ia" and sometimes the framework ia.....a tahi. For example:

> *Ia ite 'au 'ia ia, e he'e au* = When I see him , I will go

> *Ia tihe atou, a tahi tatau e kaikai* = When they come, we'll all eat.

Negation particles are:

'a'e, 'a'o'e, and umo'i – The word order changes a bit:

> *A'e 'au e ite* = I don't see, I don't know.

> *A'o'e 'au e ite* = I REALLY don't see, don't know.

> *Umo'i 'oe e tiohi* – Don't look!

The sole object of this section is to encourage you to put as much effort into speaking Marquesan as you do into trying out your French.

# English-Marquesan/French Glossary

**ache** *n* hoke *(fr)* douleur

**adz** *n* to'I; *(fr)* herminette

**afternoon** *n* avatea *(fr)* après-midi

**airplane** *n* akiona *(fr)* avion

**all** *adj* paotu *(fr)* tout

**America** *n* Henua Menike *(fr)* Amérique

**anchor** *n* katau *(fr)* ancre

**and** *conj* me *(fr)* et

**another** *adj* titahe *(fr)* encore; une autre

**appetite** *n* one (S) oke (N) *(f)* appétit

**apple** *n* apara *(f)* pomme

**August** *n* Aukuto *(fr)* août

**cabbage** *n* su *(fr) chou*

**canoe** *n* vaa *(fr)* canoë

**cap** pa'e *(fr)* casquette

**carpenter** *n* kamuta *(fr)* charpentier

**chair** *n* nohoka *(fr)* chaise

**channel** *n* tahe ia vai *(fr)* chenal

**chart** *n* parahenua *(fr)* carte marine

**Christmas** *n* Koikapo *(fr)* Noël

**city** *n* papua ha'e nui *(fr)* ville

**clean** *adj* ma *(fr)* propre

**clock** *n* motara *(fr)* horloge

**club** (big stick) *n* uu *(fr)* casse-tête

**coconut** *n* ehi *(fr)* noix de coco

**cold** *adj* metoke *(fr)* froid

**companion** *n* hoa *(fr)* compagnon

**dance** *n* haka, ori *(f)* danse (noun); danser (verb)

**danger** *n* mea hauhau *(fr)* danger

**December** *n* Teihemepere *(fr)* décembre

**deep** *adj* mea hononu *(fr)* profond

**depart** *v* ua hee *(fr)* partir

**diesel** *n* masute *(fr)* diésel

**difficult** *adj* hana nui *(fr)* difficile

**dirty** *adj* mea epo *(fr)* malpropre; sale

**dive** *v* uku *(fr)* plonger

**do** *v* hana *(fr)* faire

**dock** *n* pakatea *(fr)* dock; quai

**doctor** *n* tatihi *(fr)* docteur; médecin

**dog** *n* peto *(fr)* chien

**dollar** *n* tora *(fr)* dollar

**dolphin** *n* paaoa *(fr)* dauphin

**door** *n* avaputa *(fr)* porte

**dress** *n* ropa *(fr)* tenue

**drift** *v* ana *(fr)* driver

**drum** *n* pahu *(fr)* tambour

**drunk** *adj* kona *(fr)* ivre (or twist your nose, that's what the French do)

**East** *n* Tihana ote oumate *(fr)* est

**English** *n* Peketane *(fr)* anglais

**ear** *n* puaika *(fr)* oreille

**earth** *n* aomaama *(fr)* terre

**eat** *v* kaikai *(fr)* manger

**egg** *n* mama'i *(fr)* oeuf

**eight** *adj* eva'u *(fr)* huit

**empty** *adj* kiko ko'e *(fr)* vide

**entrance** *n* avaputa *(fr)* entrée

**error** *n* teka *(fr)* erreur

**evening** *n* ahiahi *(fr)* soir

**expensive** *adj* mea hokonui *(fr)* cher

**expert** *n* tuhuka (S) tuhuna (N) *(fr)* expert

**eyes** *n* mata *(fr)* yeux

**France** *n* Henua Farani *(fr)* France

**Friday** *n* Venini *(fr)* vendredi

**face** *n* mata *(fr)* visage

**family** *n* huaa ha'e *(fr)* famille

**fast** *adv* mea koi *(fr)* rapide

**fat** *adj* ta'uta'u *(fr)* gras; gros

**feather** *n* huu manu *(fr)* plume

**female** *n* vehine, koivi *(fr)* femme

**film** *n* e'ata *(fr)* pellicule

**finger** *n* mamaka iima *(fr)* doigt

**fish** *n* ika *(fr)* poisson

**flower** *n* pua *(fr)* fleur

**food** *n* kai *(fr)*; nourriture; provisions

**foot** *n* vae *(fr)* pied

**fork** *n* oka *(fr* fourchette

**free** *adj* tukupu *(fr)* libre

**friend** *n* hoa *(fr)* ami

**fruit** *n* puku *(fr)* fruit

**fuel** *n* masute (diesel), kasi (gasoline); *(fr)* essence; diésel

**God** *n* Etua *(fr)* Dieu

**garbage** *n* ka'u *(fr)* poubelle (garbage can); ordures (rubbish)

**garden** *n* papua *(f)* jardin

**garlic** *n* rai *(fr)* ail

**get** *v* ko'ana *(fr)*; chercher; obtenir

**gift** *n* taetea koana *(fr)* cadeau

**give** *v* tuku *(fr)* donner

**glad** *adj* koakoa *(fr)* content

**glass** *n* karahi *(fr)* verre

**go** *v* he'e *(fr)* aller

**goat** *n* keukeu *(fr)* chèvre

**good** *adj* kanahau, meitai *(fr)* bon

**goodbye** *interj., n* apa'e *(fr)* au revoir

**great** *adj* metai *(fr)* grand

**green** *adj* mea opio *(fr)* vert

**grow** *v* tupu *(fr)*; cultiver

**guitar** *n* kita *(fr)* guitare

**hammer** *n* hama *(fr)* marteau

**happy** *adj* koekoe, mamau *(fr)* content

**hard** *adj* he'o *(fr)* dur

**hat** *n* pae *(fr)* chapeau

**head** *n* upoko *(fr)* tête

**healthy** *adj* meitai *(fr)* sain

**heaven** *n* havaiki, havai'i *(fr)* paradis

**hello** *interj., n* kaoha *(fr)* bonjour

**help** *v* toko *(fr)* aider

**her** *pn* ia *(fr)* elle

**here** *adv* inei *(fr)* ici

**him** *pn* ia *(fr)* lui

**hole** *n* ua *(fr)* trou; creux

**home** *n* ha'e *(fr)* maison

**hook** *n* metau *(fr)* hameçon (fishing)

**hot** *adj* ve'ave'a *(fr)* chaud

**house** *n* ha'e *(fr)* maison

**human** *n* enana, enata *(fr)* humain

**I** *pn* oau *(fr)* moi, je

**ice** *n* vaianu, karasi *(fr)* glace

**ill** *adj* mamae *(fr)* malade

**important** *adf* taetae nui *(fr)* important

**in** *prep* i oto *(fr)* [French has many words for in, some of which occur *in* a verb; best to study your French]

**infant** tama iti *(fr)* enfant

**insect** *n* manumanu *(fr)* insect

**intelligent** *adj* maama *(fr)* intelligent

**ironwood tree** *n* toa

**it** *pron* mea

**January** *n* Ihanuario *(fr )*janvier

**journey** *n* hee *(fr)* voyage

**joy** *n* koakoa *(fr)* joie

**kava** *n* kava

**keel** *n* haatoko *(fr)* quille

**kerosene** *n* kaohenua *(fr)* kérosène

**key** *n* kiri *(fr)* clé

**kilometer** *n* kirometera *(fr)* kilomètre

**kiss** *n* hoki *(fr)* embrasser (verb); baiser; bise (noun)

**kitchen** *n* ha e kuki *(fr)* cuisine

**knee** *n* mu'o *(fr)* genou

**knife** *n* kohe *(fr)* couteau

**knot** *n* pona *(fr)* noeud

**lady** *n* vehine *(fr)* madame

**land** *n* henua (N), fenua (S) *(fr)* terre

**large** *adj* mea rui (N), mea kei (S) *(fr)* gros; grand

**laugh** *v* kata (N), ata (S) *(fr)* rire

**left** (direction) *adj* iima a 'e *(fr)* gauche

**light** *n,v* ama *(fr)* lumière

**little** *adj* mea iti *(fr)* petit

**lobster** *n* u'a *(fr)* langouste

**lunch** *(fr)* kaikai avatea *(fr)* déjeuner

**Marquesan** *n* enana (N), enata (S), *(fr)* Marquisien(ne)

**machine** *n* masini *(fr)* machine

**mail** *n* kurie *(fr)* poste

**make** *v* hana *(fr)* faire

**man** *n* vahana *(fr)* homme

**many** *adj* mea nui *(fr)* beaucoup

**map** *n* ata henua, parahenua *(fr)* carte

**marine** *adj* no te moana, no te tai *(fr)* marine

**market** *n* makete *(fr)* marché

**marvelous** *adj* kanahau pao *(fr)* merveilleux

**mast** *n* tia *(fr)* mât

**mattress** *n* peti *(fr)* matelas

**me** *pron* oua *(fr)* moi

**meal** *n* kaikai *(fr)* repas

**meat** *n* kiko *(fr)* viande

**mechanic** *n* meka *(fr)* mécanicien

**metal** *n* puhipuhi (N), paapaa (S) *(fr)* métal

**mile** *n* maire *(fr)* mille

**minute** *n* miniti *(fr)* minute

**missionary** *n* enana mitinane *(fr)* missionaire

**mistake** *n* teka *(fr)* erreur

**money** *n* moni *(fr)* argent

**month** *n* mahina (S), meama (N) *(fr)* mois

**moon** *n (same as above)* manhina (S), meama (N) *(fr)* lune

**moor** *v* vahe moo *(fr)* amarrer

**more** *adj* haka ua *(fr)* plus

**mother** *n* kui *(fr)* mère

**much** *adj* mea nui oko *(fr)* beaucoup

**my** *pron* na'u *(fr)* mon/ma

**myth** *n* akakai *(fr)* mythe

**nail** *n* paapaa, puhipuhi *(fr)* clou

**name** *n* ikoa *(fr)* nom

**near** *adj* tata *(fr)* près

**needle** *n* nina *(fr)* aiguille

**never** *adv* a'e he mea *(fr)* jamais

**night** *n* po *(fr)* soir

**no** *adv* mo'i, a'o'e *(fr)* non

**noon** *n* miti *(fr)* midi

**not** *adv* a'o'e *(fr)* non

**now** *adv* tenei *(fr)* maintenant

**oar** *n* hae *(fr)* rame

**obtain** *v* koaka *(fr)* obtenir

**ocean** *n* tai, moana *(fr)* mer

**of** *prep* no, na *(fr)* de

**oil** *n* kao *(fr)* huile

**old** *adj* kooua *(fr)* vieux (person); ancien (thing)

**on** *prep* io *(fr)* sur

**one** *adj* etahi *(fr)* un(e)

**onion** *n* aninani *(fr)* oignon

**or** *prep* u *(fr)* ou

**orange** *n* anani *(fr)* orange

**orange tree** *n* tumu anani *(fr)* oranger

**origin** *n* tumu (neat eh? An orange tree is an 'orange origin') *(fr)* origine

**out** *prep* vaho *(fr)* [most verbs contain the preposition]; outside: dehors

**oven** *n* umu *(fr)* four

**over** *prep* mauka *(fr)* au-dessus de (above)

**paddle** *n* hoe *(fr)* pagaie

**pain** *n* mamae *(fr)* douleur

**paint** *n* peni *(fr)* peindre (verb); peinture (noun)

**palm** *n* tumu ehi ("coconut origin", nice eh?) *(fr)* palmier

**paradise** *n* papua *(fr)* paradis

**paper** *n* hamani *(fr)* papier

**parents** *n* motua kui *(fr)* parents

**party** *n* koika *(fr)* réunion; soirée; célébration

**passport** *n* hamain haa *(fr)* passeport

**peace** *n* hakahau *(fr)* paix

**pearl** *n* mata uhi *(fr)* perle

**people** *n* enana, enata *(fr)* gens

**pepper** *n* neva, pepa *(fr)* poivre

**petrol** *n* kasorina *(fr)* pétrole

**physician** *n* tatihi *(fr)* médicin; docteur

**pig** *n* puaka, pua'a *(fr)* cochon

**pig dance** *n* maha'u

**place** *n* vahi *(fr)* lieu; place

**pole** *n* pou *(fr)* poteau

**porpoise** *n* paaoa *(fr)* dauphin

**potato** *n* kumaa hao'e *(fr)* pomme de terre

**pretty** (to make) *v* hakakanahau (fr) faire joli(e)

**problem** *n* kohii *(fr)* problème

**propeller** *n* pekahi *(fr)* hélice

**pump** *n* pamu *(fr)* pompe (noun); pomper (verb)

**quay** *n* pakatea *(fr)* quai

**queen** *n* haatepeiu *(fr)* reine

**quick** *adj* veve *(fr)* vite

**quiet** *adj* haka 'ea (fr)tranquil (adj) tranquillité (noun)

**radio** *n* ratio *(fr)* radio

**rag** *n* tapa *(fr)* chiffon

**rain** *n* ua *(fr)* pluie

**rat** *n* kio'e *(fr)* rat

**raw** *adj* tee, kai tee *(fr)* cru

**ray** *n* hihi *(fr)* raie

**razor** *n* kohe vau kumikumi *(fr)* rasoir

**read** *v* tetau hamani, tatau *(fr)* lire

**rear** *r* ihope, imu'i *(fr)* derrière

**reason** *n* tumu *(fr)* raison

**red** *adj* pukiki, u'au 'a, ku'a *(fr)* rouge

**reef** *n* a'ia, akau, motu one *(fr)* récif

**refrigerator** *n* firiko *(fr)* frigo

**relax** *v* haa topa te au, tukutuku *(fr)* relâcher

**religion** *v* hakaoko *(fr)* religion

**renew** *v* hakahou *(fr)* renouveler

**rent** *v,n* ai 'e tuki *(fr)* loyer

**repair** *v* kanea haka 'ua *(fr)* réparation

**request** *v* ape *(fr)* demande

**rescue** *v* toko *(fr)* sauver

**respect** *v* haapaka ihi *(fr)* respecter

**rest** *n,v* haatopa te au, hakaea *(fr)* reposer

**rib of boat** *v* vakavaka *(fr)* côte

**ripe** *adj* mea paa *(fr)* mûr

**river** *n* kaavai *(fr)* rivière

**road** *n* vaanui (N) uapu (S) *(fr)* route

**room** *n* paoto *(fr)* salle; chambre

**row** *v* pa ve'i, ho'e *(fr)* ramer

**rudder** *n* uki, ui *(fr)* gouvernail

**run** *v* vaevae oko, koi *(fr)* courir

**sad** *adj,adv* kuhane koe *(fr)* triste

**sail** *n* ka *(fr)* voile

**sailor** *n* mataro *(fr)* marin

**salt** *n* paa tai *(fr)* sel

**sandalwood** *n* puahi *(fr)* bois de santal

**Saturday** *n* Tameti *(fr)* samedi

**saw** *n* hika *(fr)* scie

**school** *n* ha'e hamani *(fr)* école

**scissor** *n* pa'oti *(fr)* ciseaux

**screw** *n,v* vis, kavii *(fr)* vis

**screwdriver** *n* turunevis *(fr)* tournevis

**sea** *n* tai *(fr)* mer

**see** *v* ite, kite *(fr)* voir

**seed** *n* kakano *(fr)* graine

**sell** *v* hano, hako *(fr)* vendre

**September** *n* Ihepetempere *(fr)* septembre

**seven** *adj* ehitu(N) efitu(S) *(fr)* sept

**seventeen** *adj* onohu a ehitu *(fr)* dix-sept

**seventy** *adj* ehitu onohu *(fr)* soixante-dix

**sew** *v* tui *(fr)* coudre

**sewing machine** *n* pariri tui kahu *(fr)* machine à coudre

**she** *pn* oia, moi *(fr)* elle

**ship** *n* ihepe *(fr)* bateau

**shirt** *n* sami *(fr)* chemise

**shop** *n* ha'e hoko, hoko *(fr)* magasin

**shore** *n* papatai, tahatai *(fr)* rivage

**shower** *n* vai kaukau *(fr)* douche

**signal** *n* hakatu *(fr)* signal

**simple** *adj* tupe paka *(fr)* simple

**sing** *v* himene *(fr)* chanter

**sink** *v* kao *(fr)* descendre

**sinker** [fishing] *n* pokae *(fr)* plomb

**sister** *n* tuehine *(fr)* soeur

**sit** *v* kapee *(fr)* s'assseoir

**six** *adj* ono *(fr)* six

**sixteen** *adj* onohu 'uu ma eono *(fr)* seize

**sixty** *adj* cono onohuu *(fr)* soixante

**sky** *n* aki,ani *(fr)* ciel

**sleep** *v,n* hiamoe *(fr)* dormir

**slow** *adj* hee mo'u *(fr)* lent

**small** *adj* iti *(fr)* petit(e)

**soap** *n* hopa(S), pu'a(N) *(fr)* savon

**son** *n* tama *(fr)* fils

**soon** *adv* po, tiaki *(fr)* bientôt

**South** *n* metaki kanauu *(fr)* sud

**sow** *n* tutu *(fr)* truie

**spectacles** *n* karahi mata *(fr)* lunettes

**spoon** *n* miti, kuiea *(fr)* cuillère

**stamp** *n* titiro, ata *(fr)* timbre

**star** *n* hetu, fetu *(fr)* étoile

**steer** *v* uki *(fr)* gouverner

**stomach** *n* kopu, kopukaikai *(fr)* estomac

**stop** *v* haka 'ea *(fr)* s'arrêter

**store** *n* ha'e hoko *(fr)* magasin

**street** *n* vaanui *(fr)* route; rue

**strong** *adj* heo, oko *(fr)* fort(e)

**sugar** *n* manini *(fr)* sucre

**summer** *n* ava ve'ave'a *(fr)* été

**sun** *n* oumati *(fr)* soleil

**Sunday** *n* atapu *(fr)* dimanche

**swim** *v* kau *(fr)* nager

**table** *n* tapu, vaina kai *(fr)* table

**tank** *n* pasa, tura(water) *(fr)* réservoir

**tap** *n* ropine(water) *(fr)* robinet

**tattoo** *n* patu tiki *(fr)* tatouage

**teeth** *n* niho *(fr)* dents

**the** *art* te *(fr)* le, la, l', les

**them, they** *pn* atou *(fr)* ils (subject only); eux (emphatic)

**third** *adj* tetou *(fr)* troisième

**thirsty** *adj* matei te mao *(fr)* soif

**Thursday** *n* Iuti, Po e ha *(fr)* jeudi

**time** *n* hora ehia *(fr)* heure (clock time); temps (general)

**tiny** *adj* pitivivi *(fr)* minuscule

**tire** *n* huira *(fr)* pneu

**to** *prep* i *(fr)* à

**today** *adv* tenei *(fr)* aujourd'hui

**toilet** *n* kapine *(fr)* toilette

**tooth** *n* niho *(fr)* dent

**tortoise** *n* honu *(fr)* tortue

**tow** *v* tavere, etoi *(fr)* remorquer

**town** *n* oire *(fr)* ville

**toy** *n* keu *(fr)* jouet

**trail** *n* vaanui iti *(fr)* chemin (path; trail)

**tree** *n* tumu *(fr)* arbre

**trousers** *n* pataro *(fr)* pantalons

**truck** *n* toroke *(fr)* camion

**Tuesday** *n* Marati *(fr)* mardi

**tuna** *n* vau, kahi *(fr)* thon

**turtle** *n* honu *(fr)* tortue

**twelve** *adj* onohuu ma ua *(fr)* douze

**twenty** *adj* tekau *(fr)* vingt

**under** *prep* maa'o *(fr)* sous

**understand** *v* vivini *(fr)* comprendre

**up** *adv* uka *(fr)* haut (high up)

**us** *prn* matou *(fr)* nous

**use** *v* haa hana *(fr)* utiliser

**vacation** *n* hakaea *(fr)* vacances

**valley** *n* kaavai *(fr)* vallée

**victuals/food** *n* o'a *(fr)* nourriture

**virgin** *n* virikine *(fr)* vierge

**visit** *v* tiheia *(fr)* visiter

**vomit** *v* haa ua *(fr)* vomir

**walk** *v* hee taha *(fr)* marcher

**want** *v* makimaki *(fr)* vouloir

**wash** (clothes) puakahu *(fr)* laver

**water** *n* vai *(fr)* eau

**waterfall** *n* vaiee *(fr)* cascade

**wave** *n* kautai *(fr)* vague

**Wednesday** *adj* Mareti *(fr)* mercredi

**we** *prn* tatou *(fr)* nous

**week** *n* tominika *(fr)* semaine

**well** *adj* meitai *(fr)* bien

**West** *adj* No'oia oumati *(fr)* ouest

**wet** *adj* paipai i te vai *(fr)* humide (damp); mouillé (wet)

**whale** *n* paaoa *(fr)* baleine

**wheel** *n* pariri ui *(fr)* roue

**Which way?** *prn* ma he'a *(fr)* quelle voie; quel chemin

**white** *adj* maita *(fr)* blanc

**why** *adv* umaha *(fr)* pourquoi

**work** *v* hana, haka *(fr)* travailler

**workshop** *n* fa'e hana *(fr)* atelier

**world** *n* aomaama nei *(fr)* monde

**wreck** *v* haa hatarara *(fr)* détruire

**wrench** *n* kavii oko *(fr)* clé anglaise

**write** *v* patu i te hamani *(fr)* écrire

**yacht** *n* iake *(fr)* yacht

**yard** *n* papua ha'e *(fr)* cour; jardin

**yeast** *n* haapupuhi *(fr)* levure

**yellow** *adj* putokatoka *(fr)* jaune

# Appendix D
# RECIPES

Marquesans are the gourmets of Polynesia. Of course, that title might be decided by individual taste, but all the edible plants and animals of the archipelago are prepared and consumed with gusto. Western tastes do not generally migrate toward uncooked meat but nothing compares to "Poisson cru" (uncooked fish) as prepared by the Marquesans. Octopus is prepared much in the same way with the addition of some hefty bashing on the reef to tenderize it. When prepared correctly, the octopus will taste similar to shrimp.

They lose me only when eating the little crabs that inhabit the reef. They eat them raw with a little lime juice but unfortunately for me and fortunately for the crabs, there isn't enough lime juice in the world to mitigate that low-tide flavor. Lime juice and coconut milk are used extensively and, in the case of lime juice, constitutes the "stove top" for many foods. A fisherman or a hunter will go out for the day with nothing more in his pocket but a few limes which he will squeeze over a fish he caught (or the bait he uses). The acid in the juice will "cook" the meat, turn it opaque and add a unique flavor to a simple dish. *Bon appétit!*

# "World Famous" Marquesan Poisson Cru

Some recipes are tolerant of deviations in ingredients. These recipes must be followed to the letter to achieve the best results.

**Tuna** - get up at 2 a.m. and go catch a big tuna. Next, cut off all the unappealing parts of the fish. We don't want any eyes, viscera, skin or bones, just one kilo of nice tuna meat. Cut the tuna into pieces about the size of 1/2 of your little finger or maybe a little bigger or a little smaller. Accuracy is important.

**Limes** – borrow about 40 limes from a friendly Marquesan's backyard tree. Squeeze the limes through a sieve into a separate bowl. We don't want seeds!

**Vegetables** - go down to the marché and trade a box of .22 shells for a bunch of veggies—two cukes, a few tomatoes, an onion or two, bell peppers (two colors if possible) and even a few celery stalks would be nice.

**Coconuts** - climb a coconut tree and get a couple of ripe coconuts. No green ones, please. They are good for drinking, but not for copra. If you survive the fall, shuck the nut, crack it in half with a machete and use a *rapacoco* to shred it. A *rapacoco* is a toothed metal device that makes short work of a coconut. You can get one at Kamake's or Maurice's in Taiohae and other places around the island. The meat must be finely shredded. (André at the marché will grind up your coconut on his new-fangled mechanical coconut grinder if you enjoy bucking tradition.)

Cut up the veggies into bite-sized pieces and slice the onion very, very, *very* thin. The next part is the most critical part of the operation. Pour the lime juice over the tuna and stir it up with your hands. Let the tuna "cook" unheated in the lime juice for between five minutes and two hours. It's your call, but the timing is crucial. The meat should turn slightly opaque. If you borrowed over-ripe limes, you could cook it for a year and nothing would happen except putrefaction. (You can use the yellow, over-ripe ones in rum and coke drinks but not for tuna.) Once the cooking is complete, drain the excess lime juice and throw a tablespoon of white pepper in with the veggies.

# Lime juice

This recipe is not Marquesan at all. Since the islands are bursting with lime trees, the Marquesans have no need to preserve the juice. For cruisers, on the other hand, it is a treat to be able to carry lime juice on long voyages without it spoiling.

This procedure was taught to me by Tracey Smith who, after years of cruising around the world, has settled on Nuku Hiva. She is very active on the island as an aerobics instructor, English teacher, para-gliding enthusiast and tamuré dancer.

Wash and dry as many Mason jars as you think you will need. After squeezing the juice, put it in an appropriately sized pot and place it on the stove. Add a cup of sugar for every cup of juice and heat until you see the first signs of simmering. Do not boil. Pour juice into the mason jars and cap them. When they cool the lids should become concave and will remain preserved for several months. (Add a vanilla bean—available in Taipivai—to each jar and the flavor will be further enhanced.)

To make limeade, add four tablespoons of the concentrate to an eight-ounce glass of water and ice. You'll probably want to add some more sugar too.

# Chèvre au Lait Coco

There is a certain similarity between this recipe and my "World Famous Poisson Cru Recipe." You will probably notice the two main differences right off the bat. One, we're fixing goat meat, not fish. Two, we will cook the goat with heat from a stove, not with lime juice (this is not Goat Cru). Now that everything is clear, whip out your pots and pans and off we go.

First (this will be familiar), go out and butcher a goat. If this doesn't work, get a Marquesan friend to do it for you. Young goat is preferable. For this recipe you need only one hind leg. As you did with my "World Famous Poisson Cru" recipe, get rid of everything unappetizing, i.e., skin, fur, etc. You might want your Marquesan friend to do this part also. Cut the meat off the bone in one- to two-inch chunks.

Toss the meat into your pressure cooker. Throw in the leg bone too. Cover the meat with water and bring to a boil. Just sit there and let it boil for 15 or 20 minutes unpressurized. Now, with a colander, drain all the water off. Toss the meat back into the pressure cooker. Then throw in two chopped onions, three minced garlic cloves, a tablespoon of salt and a teaspoon of black pepper. Put two inches of fresh water in the bottom of the cooker and pressure cook (valve spinning) for 20 minutes.

Let off the steam and add a couple cups of coconut milk and heat to a boil. (See my "World Famous Poisson Cru Recipe" for details on making coconut milk.) Remove from the heat and serve with *me'i*, taro, tarua or rice.

# Pig Roast (Puaka)

First let's dig a pit in the sand about 3.5 feet in diameter and 18 inches deep. Obviously, it would be wise to dig the hole above the highwater mark. Fill the hole with wood and kindling and lava stones about twice the size of a softball. If

you substitute other rocks for lava stones, they may blow up which could spoil your afternoon. Light the fire and allow it to burn until only coals are left when the pyre is leveled. Then, lay two-foot strips of quartered banana tree trunks parallel to each other, nearly covering the stones. Place a one-inch thick layer of breadfruit (*me'i*) leaves atop the banana trunk spacers.

Now it gets serious. You will need one or two 30- to 35-pound porkers. Take all the hair off; entrails are also unacceptable. The head and tail stays. Now put the piggies spread-eagle on the *me'i* (*may-ee*) leaves along with a bunch of bananas. Cover these guys with two or three layers of banana leaves then two layers of burlap bags. Spread sand on the edges of the burlap to keep the smoke in and air out. Cover any place you see smoke escaping with earth or sand.

In four hours start uncovering the *puaka* and enjoy. They will be tender and juicy and the bananas will be cooked *parfaitement!*

# Popoi Mei and Popoi Manioc

Popoi is a starchy staple, in one form or another, enjoyed by most of the Maori populations throughout the Pacific. The basis for popoi is breadfruit. Breadfruit is fermented and aged into "ma." First, pick the breadfruit and hang it for two days. Remove the skin and cores. In ancient times, pits were dug, lined with pandanus or palm leaves, and breadfruit was thrown in and stomped. This preservation process guarded against famine should there be a decline in breadfruit production. The "ma" was, and is, allowed to ferment and dry for as long as a year.

When popoi was desired, the dry ma was dug from the pit and fresh breadfruit (*me'i*) was added along with some water. It was mixed up and the whole gelatinous mass plopped onto a deep tray and to be eaten with the fingers. (A similar dish, Ka'aku, is beaten, ripe, cooked breadfruit paste with coconut mild added.)

Popoi is also made by substituting manioc flour (tapioca) for the fresh me'i.

No matter how you prepare popoi, it is always eaten with the fingers. The hand is arranged like the Boy Scout salute with the index and middle fingers together. The fingers are dipped into the popoi and withdrawn with a flourish and a twist to keep the goo on the fingers during the trip to the mouth.

Author sketch of breadfruit

# MILEAGE GUIDE

*Mileage in Nautical Miles.*
*Headings are Magnetic and direct, as the Pitaki bird flies.*

## The Marquesas Islands

| FROM: \ TO: | ANAHO NUKU HIVA | ANSE DESANIS TAHUATA | BAIE D'HANE UA HUKA | HAKAHAU UA POU | HAKAHETAU UA POU | HAKATEA NUKU HIVA | HANAIAPA HIVA OA | HANAMENU HIVA OA |
|---|---|---|---|---|---|---|---|---|
| Anaho/Nuku Hiva | | 88.4/130° | 32.1/091° | 32.1/168° | 32.2/174° | 9.4/208° | 82./120° | 78.6/125° |
| Anse Desanis/Tahuata | 88.4/310° | | 66.6/327° | 66.6/292° | 68.9/291° | 86.9/304° | 15.9/011° | 12.0/343° |
| Baie d'Hane/Ua Huka | 32.1/271° | 66.6/148° | | 39.9/219° | 42.5/222° | 37.3/258° | 56.1/136° | 55.2/144° |
| Hakahau/Ua Pou | 32.1/348° | 66.0/113° | 39.9/039° | | 3.4/260° | 25.7/334° | 64.8/099° | 59.0/283° |
| Hakahetau/Ua Pou | 32.2/354 | 68.9/111° | 42.5/042° | 3.4/180° | | 25.0/342° | 68.0/098° | 62.2/102 |
| Hakatea/Nuku Hiva | 9.4/028° | 86.9/124° | 37.3/078° | 25.7/154° | 25.0/162° | | 82.2/114° | 78.0/118° |
| Hana Iapa/Hiva Oa | 81.9/300° | 15.9/191° | 56.3/316° | 64.7/279° | 68.0/278° | 82.2/293° | | 7.8/238 |
| Hana Menu/Hiva Oa | 78.6/305° | 12.0/163° | 55.2/324° | 59.0/283° | 62.2/282° | 78.0/298 | 7.8/058° | |
| Hana Moe Noa/Tahuata | 86.8/308° | 3.0/187° | 64.3/326° | 65.2/290° | 68.2/288° | 85.6/302° | 12.9/012° | 9.3/335° |
| Hana Vave/Fatu Hiva | 128.3/310° | 39.8/308° | 105.1/320° | 104.8/298° | 107.5/297° | 126.7/305° | 49.2/325° | 50.2/316° |
| Ivaiva/Tahuata | 86.9/309° | 2.7/185° | 64.5/326° | 65.2/290° | 68.2/289° | 85.7/302° | 13.2/013° | 9.6/337° |
| Taahuku/Hiva Oa | 84.9/303° | 10.7/197° | 60.3/320° | 65.8/283° | 69.0/282° | 84.5/297° | 5.4/359° | 6.8/280° |
| Taiohae/Nuku Hiva | 6.3/013° | 85.8/126° | 34.0/081° | 26.6/162° | 26.4/169° | 3.7/234° | 80.4/116° | 76.5/121 |
| Taipivai/Nuku Hiva | 6.4/323° | 82.2/129° | 28.6/081° | 26.5/173° | 26.9/181° | 8.8/249° | 76.2/118° | 76.5/121° |
| Vaiehu/Oa Pou | 34.1/356° | 69.2/109° | 44.8/042° | 5.2/060° | 2.3/029° | 26.6/345° | 68.9/096° | 62.9/100° |
| Vaitahu/Tahuata | 87.5/309° | 1.4/179° | 65.4/327° | 65.4/291° | 68.3/290° | 86.1/303° | 14.5/012° | 10.6/340° |
| Vaituha/Eiao | 62.0/132 | 150.4/131° | 88.8/118° | 90.0/144° | 88.6/146° | 64.9/140° | 143.3/126° | 140.4/128° |

# The Marquesas Islands

Continued

| FROM: \ TO: | HANA MOE NOA TAHUATA | HANAVAVE FATU HIVA | IVAIVA TAHUATA | TAAHUKU HIVA OA | TAIOHAE HIVA OA | TAIPIVAI NUKU HIVA | VAIEHU UA POU | VAITAHU TAHUATA | VAITUHA EIAO |
|---|---|---|---|---|---|---|---|---|---|
| Anaho/Nuku Hiva | 86.8/128° | 128.3/130° | 86.9/129° | 84.9/123° | 6.3/193° | 6.4/143° | 34.1/176° | 87.5/129° | 62.0/312° |
| Anse Desanis/Tahuata | 3.0/007° | 39.8/129° | 2.7/005° | 10.7/017° | 85.8/306° | 82.2/309° | 69.2/289° | 1.4/359° | 150.4/310° |
| Baie d'Hane/Ua Huka | 64.3/146° | 105.1/141° | 64.5/146° | 60.3/140° | 34.0/261° | 28.6/261° | 44.8/222° | 65.4/147° | 88.8/298° |
| Hakahau/Ua Pou | 65.2/110° | 104.8/119° | 65.2/110° | 65.8/103° | 26.6/342° | 26.5/353° | 5.2/240° | 65.4/112° | 90.0/324° |
| Hakahetau/Ua Pou | 68.2/109 | 107.5/118° | 68.2/109° | 69.0/102° | 26.4/349° | 26.9/001° | 2.3/209° | 68.3/110° | 88.6/326° |
| Hakatea/Nuku Hiva | 85.6/122° | 126.7/126° | 85.7/122° | 84.5/117° | 3.7/054° | 8.8/069° | 26.6/165° | 86.1/123° | 64.9/320° |
| Hanaiapa/Hiva Oa | 13.9/192 | 49.2/145° | 13.2/193° | 5.4/179° | 80.4/296° | 76.2/298° | 68.9/276° | 14.5/192° | 143.2/305° |
| Hana Menu/Hiva Oa | 9.3/155° | 50.2136° | 9.6/157° | 6.8/100° | 76.5/301° | 72.5/303° | 62.9/280° | 10.6/161° | 140.4/308° |
| Hana Moe Noa/Tahuata | | 41.5/132° | 0.4/200° | 7.7/021° | 84.3/304° | 80.6/307° | 68.6/286° | 1.6/193° | 148.7/309° |
| Hanavave/Fatu Hiva | 41.5/312° | | 41.4/311° | 44.9/321° | 125.6/307° | 122.0/129° | 107.6/296° | 40.8/310° | 190.2/310° |
| Ivaiva/Tahuata | 0.4/020° | 41.4/132° | | 8.1/021° | 84.4/304 | 80.7/307° | 68.6/287° | 1.2/191° | 148.9/310° |
| Taahuku/Hiva Oa | 7.7/201° | 44.9/141° | 8.1/201° | | 82.9/299° | 78.9/301° | 69.7/280° | 9.3/200° | 146.5/307° |
| Taiohae/Nuku Hiva | 84.3/125° | 125.6/127° | 84.4/125° | 82.9/119° | | 5.3/080° | 28.2/172° | 84.9/126° | 65.2/317° |
| Taipivai/Nuku Hiva | 80.6/127° | 122.0/129° | 80.7/127° | 78.9/122° | 5.3/260° | | 29.0/183° | 81.3/128° | 68.3/313° |
| Vaiehu/Ua Pou | 68.6/107° | 107.6/116° | 68.6/107° | 69.7/100° | 28.2/352° | 29.0/003° | | 68.7/108° | 89.7/327° |
| Vaitahu/Tahuata | 1.6/013° | 40.8/130° | 1.2/011° | 9.3/020° | 84.9/305° | 81.3/308° | 68.7/288° | | 149.5/310° |
| Vaituha/Eiao | 148.7/130° | 190.2/131° | 148.9/130° | 146.5/127° | 65.2/137° | 68.3/133° | 89.7/147° | 149.5/131° | |

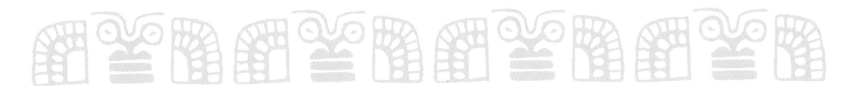

# Travel
# to the
# Marquesas
# Islands

| FROM: | TO: TAAHUKU (HIVA OA) | TAIOHAE (NUKU HIVA) |
|---|---|---|
| **ALASKA** | | |
| Juneau | 4086/158° | 4036/160° |
| Anchorage | 4286/145° | 4227/146° |
| **CANADA** | | |
| Victoria, B.C. | 3583/178° | 3545/179° |
| **U.S. WEST COAST** | | |
| Seattle | 3557/180° | 3520/181° |
| Portland | 3424/181° | 3388/182° |
| San Francisco | 2980/187° | 2950/188° |
| Los Angeles | 2954/195° | 2931/197° |
| San Diego | 2834/197° | 2814/199° |
| **MEXICO** | | |
| Ensenada | 2779/198° | 2761/200° |
| La Paz | 2639/213° | 2639/215° |
| **PANAMA** | | |
| Canal Zone | 3718/255° | 3765/256° |
| **ECUADOR** | | |
| Galapagos Islands | 3002/252° | 3059/254° |
| Guayaquil | 3582/258° | 3640/259° |
| **PACIFIC** | | |
| Pitcairn | 1081/315° | 1157/314° |
| Tuamotu | 579/039° | 571/031° |
| Papeete | 769/042° | 756/036° |
| Tonga | 2101/067° | 2058/065° |
| Fiji | 2347/070° | 2301/068° |
| Wellington, NZ | 3082/044° | 3076/042° |
| Honolulu | 2165/137° | 2087/137° |

# Recommended References

*Charlie's Charts of Polynesia,* Charles E. Wood, 4th Edition, rev. by Margo Wood (Charlie's Charts, 2000)

*Les Derniers Sauvages,* Max Radiguet (Les Editions du Pacific, 1981)

*A Dream of Islands,* Daws (W.W. Norton, 1980)

*Encyclopédie de la Polynésie,* C. Gleral (Multi Press, 1986)

*Exotic Plant Manual,* Graf (Roehrs Company, 1974, third edition)

*Forever the Land of Men*: *An Account of a Visit to the Marquesas Islands,* Willowdean Handy (Dodd, Mead & Company, 1965)

*The Happy Isles of Oceania,* Paul Theroux (Fawcett, 1993)

*Hidden Worlds of Polynesia: The Chronicle of an Archeological Expedition to Nuku Hiva in the Marquesas Islands,* Robert Suggs (Harcourt, Brace & World, 1962)

*Island Civilizations of Polynesia,* Robert C. Suggs (New American Library—Mentor Series, 1960)

*Mahina Tiare,* Barbara Marrett & John Neal (Pacific International Publishing, 1993)

*Marquesan Sexual Behavior: An Anthropological Survey of Polynesian Practices,* Robert Suggs (Harcourt, Brace & World, 1966)

*Marquesan/English Dictionary,* Hokaupoko & Russell (Pauka Fio Press, 1995)

*Mave Mai—The Marquesas Islands,* Sharon Chester, Heidi Baumgartner, Diana Freshoso & James Oetzel (The Wandering Albatross, 1998)

*Moeurs et Coutumes des Anciens Maoris des Iles Marquises,* Dr. Louis Rollin (Stepolde, 1974, Papeete)

*Mutiny on the Bounty,* Nordhoff & Hall (Little, Brown & Company, 1962)

*Noa Noa, A Tahitian Journal,* Paul Gauguin (Dover Press, 1985)

*Pacific Wanderer,* Earl R. Hinz (Westcott Cove Publishing Company, 1991)

*Thunder From the Sea* (Australian National University Press, 1973)

*Typee,* Herman Melville (out of print)

*Woman Aboard,* Janet Stevenson (Chandler & Sharp, 1981)

## Acknowledgments

The people whose names I mention here are kind and giving folks who were of inestimable help in helping me plan our cruises, helping me write this book or in offering Marquesan hospitality. In case you run into any of these wonderful people, you will know that you are in the presence of true sailors and gentlepeople. I count them among my treasured friends.

Starting in the States, Denny and Steffie Philip aboard *Spellbound* were instrumental in helping me purchase and outfit *Christina*. They supported our efforts throughout the preparation period and did yeomen's duty getting a handheld replaced for us while we were "stuck" in paradise and they were still in Marina del Rey, California. I'm happy to say that Denny, Steffie and *Spellbound* are now cruising where the air is warm and skin is brown.

Thanks also to Linda Barney, a brilliant California attorney, who edited my first *Cruising World* pieces. Without her wise counsel and liberal use of the blue pencil, I would never have attempted this project.

Similarly, without developmental editor and book designer Pam Hidaka's help in separating the wheat from the chaff, this book would have ventured far and wide with no visible means of support.

Don and Réanne Douglass, my publishers, have been unflagging in their support of this book and for that I am grateful.

Mike Mandernach aboard *Goatlocker,* now happily ensconced in Australia, was invaluable in getting *Christina* ready in Marina del Rey and Ensenada.

Roy Starkey aboard *Sea Loone*, an owner-built ferro-cement 28-foot Contest, is a true sea-gypsy. I originally met Roy in the British Virgin Islands after his first circumnavigation. It was his wise counsel that we skip the Mexican Riviera and sail non-stop, instead, to the Marquesas. Roy sets an example of cruising freedom, thrift and self-sufficiency that is hard to measure up to. I credit the general flow of fair winds I have enjoyed during my years of sailing to a tiny rosewood tiki he gave me as a talisman.

Tracey Smith Tavira is now living on Nuku Hiva with her husband Joseph and their three children. I first met Tracey when she was aboard *Sea Loone* as Roy Starkey's first mate, and she has given me indispensable advice on cruising and living in the Marquesas ever since. Fritz Seyfarth, to whom this book is dedicated, "adopted" Tracey as a daughter when she and Roy cruised into Marina Cay from South Africa in the mid-1980s. Her help in keeping this book current was, and will continue to be, vital to its accuracy.

The Gendron family of Nuku Hiva are a large, warm and giving family that kept *Christina* and her crew supplied with indefatigable friendship. Adolph Gendron, a former chief administrator of Nuku Hiva, and his wife Josephine supplied hours of hospitality and tons of food during frequent meals (*kaikai's*) at their home. An avid farmer, Adolph supplied the expertise and livestock for one of the more memorable going-away beach parties that were thrown for *Christina's* crew. The roast pig-in-a-pit preparation in the Recipes section came from Adolph.

Bruno Gendron, a nephew of Adolph, and his beautiful wife Gloria, run the Nuku Hiva Village Hotel. They were generous with their time when I most needed it. One of the most valuable favors that Bruno did for me was to let me use his freezer for the storage of my tunas. How I got the tunas is explained below.

Raymond and Jeanne Gendron are the cream of a bumper crop of Gendrons! Raymond is a fishermen's fisherman. Some people say that his wife Jeanne is even better. They go out at 2 a.m. in their little boat and are back by 6 a.m. to sell the fish on the dock. Sometimes when Jeanne felt like sleeping in, Raymond would take me instead. He'd knock on the side of the boat at 2 a.m. and off we'd go into the black, black night, and I was always rewarded with a large yellow-fin tuna for my efforts. Unfortunately, the sharks usually ate more of the tuna on my line than I was able to pull aboard.

Many other Gendrons who were like family to me have married names now and will be mentioned later on.

The Leau Choy family is special, and I could never repay their kindness. Months of meals in their compound behind Magasin Kamake proved to be some of the most wonderful moments of our stay. Kamake and his wife, Mareta, provided us with food, shelter and a warm family whenever they thought we might want them. We plugged my old Pfaff sewing machine into a socket upstairs and fixed sails and awnings; Mareta cooked; we worked in the store when their son and daughter–in-law were away in Tahiti; Mareta cooked; we sold a couple of million of Kamake's Nuku Hiva T-shirts to the unsuspecting passengers on the *Darwin Explorer* (Eco-cruise ship) when it came through with a passenger load of gringos; Mareta cooked; we celebrated the renewal of vows of their oldest son, Maurice, and his wife Mary-Louise [Gendron, daughter of Adolph and Josephine]; we were part of their family and still Mareta cooked.

The Marquesan equivalent of the dinner bell is the cry, "Kaikai!" To this day I salivate when I hear, "Kaikai!" We still feel a part of the

Leau Choy family: sons Christian, Tieri, and Maurice; daughter Mary-Helen and husband Fred; grandchildren Adolph, Jessica, Jason and the new baby.

On one 5th of May, the cruisers in Taiohae decided to hold a Cinco de Mayo party at Nuku Hiva Village. It was appropriate as Cinco de Mayo celebrates a Mexican military victory over French invaders back in years of yore. During the celebration, Mary-Louise arrived and handed me a four-foot long package wrapped in old newspaper. Inside was a beautiful solid rosewood casse-tête (Marquesan war club) carved by her grandfather; only one of two that he sculpted. It resides in a display case in my home, a constant reminder of the friendship and kindness of Mary-Louise and her family.

And then, of course, there's Rose Corser, the unofficial cruising-boat-greeter on the island, and the only American citizen that I know that lives in the Marquesas . . . legally. Though the Keikehanui Inn which she once owned has now been converted to a four-star hotel complex replete with pool, she still lives in the house at the bottom of hill next to Nuku Hiva Village. I built a bungalow for Rose while I was there but it has been torn down to make room for the new resort.

Eric and Sue VanHammersveld, of *Te'ama,* were our companions for months while we researched this book. Eric is a professional graphic artist and video producer and Sue is professionally patient with Eric. Eric's presentation on holography was wildly successful at St. Anne's School on Hiva Hoa and is fondly remembered to this day. Eric and Sue, both ham radio operators. were the main contributors to the Ham Radio section of this book.

Companions and cruising buddies, Mike and Karen McNamera, aboard *Irish Mist,* a DownEaster 38 like our *Christina* had first cruised in the Marquesas 20 years earlier as newlyweds. They were of great help in providing information on the southern group of the archipelago. Unfortunately *Irish Mist* was lost on a storm-tossed reef in the Society Islands, but all hands were saved.

André and Juliette Vai'a'anui of Baie Anaho, along with their sons Teiki and Leo, and Teiki's beautiful wife, Louise, always welcomed us with open arms. There was always a cold Hinano and a ready smile for our stays in Anaho. Teiki's delicious homegrown vegetables were indispensable especially when we used Anaho as our jump-off point to Hawaii.

Justin and Julienne (I never learned their last names) live in Taiohae and have opened up their home many times to cruisers, Justin carved a tabletop for me out of a piece of teak plywood which now serves as an end table in my home—another reminder of the kindness of the Marquesans.

Lovely Deborah Kimitete, the wife of the mayor of Taiohae, and an activist for Marquesan tourism, was a fountain of information and maps. Once I "gave" her kids a kitten, much to her chagrin, and she named it after me.

In Hakahetau (Ua Pou), Etienne and Ivonne Hokaupoko held a birthday party for my first mate. A finely woven straw hat that Ivonne made is a cherished memento to this day. I have Etienne to thank for helping put together the glossary for this book

On Hiva Oa, Philippe and Pascal Lemaire, both teachers at St. Anne's (Ecole des Soeurs) gave me invaluable information about Hiva Oa and its environs. They arrived on the island aboard their own boat and settled in, and adopted a beautiful baby girl.

Serge Vai'e'enui and his family, who were gracious hosts while we were in Hana Vane, spent hours taking us up to the falls. I look forward to visiting them again soon.

Last but certainly not least, I must mention the kind friends of the Hawaii Yacht Club. We arrived unannounced at the Aloha Dock of the yacht club one New Year's Eve, after a 19-day pounding from Anaho, and were met by Richard Aly, a tall, wiry man who simply smiled and said, "Aloha. Park it here and come to the bar for a drink." At that time, there could have been no words more welcome to our ears and, for our entire time in Hawaii (which turned out to be years), the Hawaii Yacht Club members became our best friends and supporters. There are too many to mention but Patty Deacon always made us feel at home even before we were members. The late Doug Vann, another true sailor, and his wife, Sherry, made our lives richer by supporting all our efforts, nautical or otherwise.

To each and every one, I say thanks Aloha, and Kaoha!

*Joe Russell*
*Half Moon Bay, California*

# Index

*Page numbers in boldface refer to map diagrams.*

# Archaeology Index

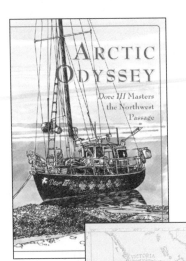

# Enjoy these other adventure books from FineEdge.com

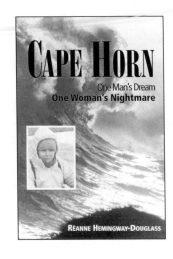

### Arctic Odyssey

Len Sherman

The account of Dove III's epic voyage through the Northwest Passage—one of the first west-to-east single-year passages on record.

### Cape Horn

**One Man's Dream, One Woman's Nightmare**

Réanne Hemingway-Douglass

"This is the sea story to read if you read only one."

—*McGraw Hill, Interntl. Marine Catalog*

### Trekka Round the World

John Guzzwell

"John Guzzwell is an inspiration to all blue-water sailors." —*Wooden Boat*

"A classic of small boat voyaging." —*Pacific Yachting*

### Final Voyage of the Princess Sophia

**Did they all have to die?**

Betty O'Keefe and Ian Macdonald

This story explores the heroic efforts of those who answered the SOS, at first to save and later to recover the bodies of those lost.

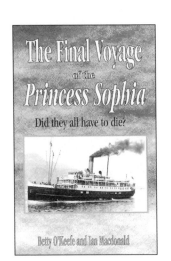

### Sea Stories of the Inside Passage

Iain Lawrence

"I can't wait to read Iain's next sea story; he describes the life of the Inside Passage like no one else." —*Sherrill and Rene Kitson, Ivory Island Lightstation*

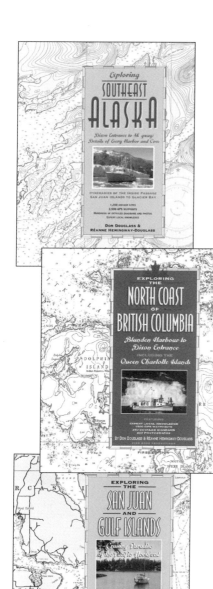

### Exploring Southeast Alaska
**Dixon Entrance to Skagway**

Don Douglass and Réanne Hemingway-Douglass

Over 1500 anchor sites in Alaska's breathtaking southeastern archipelago; for pleasurable cruising to thousands of islands and islets, deeply-cut fjords, tidewater glaciers and icebergs.

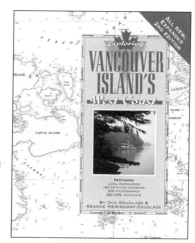

### Exploring Vancouver Island's West Coast—Second Edition

Don Douglass and Réanne Hemingway-Douglass

With five great sounds, sixteen major inlets, and an abundance of wildlife, the largest island on the west coast of North America is a cruising paradise.

### Exploring the North Coast of British Columbia

Don Douglass and Réanne Hemingway-Douglass

The ultimate pilothouse resource for exploring the beautiful northern coast of British Columbia; navigate with confidence among thousands of unnamed islands, deep fjords and the magnificent Queen Charlotte Islands.

### Exploring the South Coast of British Columbia—Second Edition
**Gulf Islands and Desolation Sound to Port Hardy and Blunden Harbour**

Don Douglass and Réanne Hemingway-Douglass

"Clearly the most thorough, best produced and most useful [of the guides] available . . . particularly well thought out and painstakingly researched." —*NW Yachting*

### Exploring the San Juan and Gulf Islands
**Cruising Paradise of the Pacific Northwest**

Don Douglass and Réanne Hemingway-Douglass

Contributors: Anne Vipond, Peter Fromm, & Warren Miller
"Another masterpiece in the exploring series . . ."

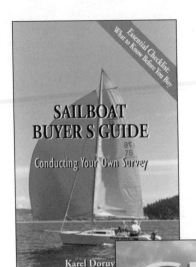

## Sailboat Buyers Guide

Karel Doruyter

How to Conduct Your Own Survey
An essential checklist for knowing before you buy!

## The Arctic to Antarctica

Mladen Sutej

The dramatic account of the first circumnavigation of the
North and South American continents—from the Northwest
Passage to the Antarctic peninsula.

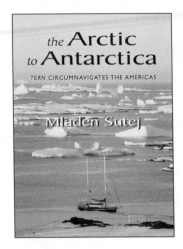

## GPS Instant Navigation

*A Practical Guide from Basics to Advanced Techniques*

Kevin Monahan and Don Douglass

"Helps get more from your navigation."—*Pacific Yachting*

"I strongly recommend this book."—*John Neal, Bluewater sailor, Mahina Tiare*

## Proven Cruising Routes

Kevin Monahan and Don Douglass

A route guide with precise courses, diagrams and GPS waypoints from Seattle to Ketchikan.

FineEdge.com
Phone (360) 299-8500 • Email: mail@FineEdge.com

*For our full catalog, check our website: www.FineEdge.com*